MERLIN'S
BOOK OF
MAGICK
AND
ENCHANTMENT

NEVILL DRURY

MetroBooks

WHAT MAY BE FOUND
WITHIN THIS BOOK
OF MAGICK

@

MAGICKAL KNOWLEDGE

@

THE MAGICK OF ENCHANTMENT

MAY I BE AN ISLAND IN THE SEA

MAY I BE A HILL ON THE LAND

MAY I BE A STAR IN THE DARK TIME

HERE

BEGINNETH

THIS BOOK

OF MAGICK...

how i came to have my magickal powers

@

Here before you now is my book of magick and wonderment – a tract of mysteries and spells and secrets, whereof some hath spoken but few have taken unto their hearts and souls. And I leave this book with you lest my learning upon the mystic Path of Magick be lost forever.

For it is surely true that these mysteries have come forth from the earth and sky, from the forests and the mountain streams. And this magick is the magick of my people, of my forefathers and womenfolk. This is magick from the dawn of the first times – magick which sings true, and whose echoes whisper through the ages. This is magick that others have perchance lost or forgotten – and so it is that I bequeath it here to you.

My name is Merlin – many know me by that name – and so too am I also called Myrddin or Merlinus Ambrosius. Some also call me mad – possessed by spirits and intoxicated by demons. Some have asked why it is that I prefer to haunt the craggy mountains or take refuge in caves. Or why it is that I love the depths of the forests and the solitary life of a wanderer. For it is true – I find my happiness and my strength in the life of a

This is magick from the dawn of the first times...

recluse. Indeed I liketh best to be by myself, alone with my wild thoughts and my haunted songs, but in truth never am I really alone. For I find my company amidst the chirpings of the raven, in the dance of the blue butterfly, in the graceful prancings of the deer, and in the distant rumblings of dragons. As night falls, then do I become drowsy and yield to the radiance of the inner world – and my mind becometh enchanted by the strange journeys of the soul. I wander through many lands and ages, and speak with birds and animals of this world and the next. There do I meet my spirit-helpers in the ways of magick, and I receiveth my knowledge from the Ancient Ones who once walked upon this earth – those who were called to the Path of Mysteries, did conjure its spells and secrets, and who now dwell in the timeless lands beyond the Veil of Mist.

But more shall I tell you of who I am, and how I came to this calling in the ways of magick and enchantment...

For it is said that my spirit-father was indeed the Devil himself, and that he sought to wreak havoc on a world where prophets, kings and emperors wished with their arrogance to become as powerful as he – to usurp his rightful role as Lord of Magick and Host of the Forces of the Night. And so did he curse those who had forgotten the old ways of Nature, and he did wish

mightily for a son who would lead the world away from sanctimonious righteousness and back to the forgotten paths of magick. And so it came to pass that my spirit-father did sow his seed in this world and then take his leave to the nether-regions. In this way was his magick born again into the world and thus did it spread to many distant realms — nurtured and reawakened all the while by those who could hear his whisperings in the wind. I, Merlin, prophet of the depths, am his spirit-son. My soul doth sing both unto the Heavens and in the dark recesses of the Earth.

But what of my mother? I knew not her name, for soon after I was born and nursed did she retreat unto a life of religious penance. But this much is clear — that all are agreed that she was an innocent maiden who until my birth had lived a simple life, both pure and good. And it is said that once my spirit-father had espied her, and sought to make her his lover, he did fill her dreams with ribald thoughts and visions of sensual pleasures. Now, for her part, my mother was troubled by these visions and these passions and in haste did seek counsel from a kindly priest named Blaise, who urged her strongly — her soul for to protect — to make the sign of the cross before going to sleep at night and before rising for her work each day. One night, though, did she take herself to sleep without making all around her the sign of the cross, and my spirit-father hath seized this time to be with her alone, within the half-light of her room.

Thus did he conjure his being into the form of a handsome priest and appear before her as a counsellor and as a friend. And soon hath he entranced her with his gentle whisperings of spiritual love and companionship. But having cast aside her fears, now did he begin to entrance her with sensual caresses, awakening in her feelings and emotions not glimpsed before. And yielding to his advances, my mother did then spend the night within his arms – her body folding into his – and by morning time the magick deed was done. Yet when she did awake there was no person to be seen and only then did she realise that unbeknownst to her perchance she had fallen prey to lovemaking with the Devil. Then with haste did she seek counsel with Blaise – for to put herself at ease that this too was a dark imagining in her mind – but to no avail. For the priest did confirm her fears and hath told her she must surely now be pregnant with this evil seed – that in due course would she give birth to the Devil's child.

And so it came to pass that I was born. It is said that when I nestled at her breast I was a cheerful, smiling child with chubby cheeks – a delight for any mother and a source of great pride and joy. And Blaise did then baptise me, so to annul the hold of the Devil and to lay to rest those demons who still lay claim to my soul. But though I was of happy disposition, many thought that I was somewhat strange in my appearance. People who took me in their arms did say quietly to one another

I did like greatly to take myself away
and make my explorations within the forest all alone...

that at times they glimpsed an ancient, restless soul residing within this baby's body – that my eyes, whilst full of life and radiance, yet also showed a depth and mystery that were not of this world. And my body was covered in soft black down, like that of a young bird. So they named me Merlin – which means 'blackbird'.

After this, and perhaps to atone for her terrible transgressions in the way of virtue, my mother did spend much of her time within the convent walls, praying and making peace with her God. Meantime, Blaise hath fathered me as best he could. And so it was that my early years were spent more with the farm animals or wandering alone in the countryside, than playing with the other children in the village. Even though quite young, I did like greatly to take myself away and make my explorations within the forest all alone. For I never was afraid. Sometimes indeed would I rest upon a bed of fallen leaves – and rabbits, foxes and badgers would then come close by, as curious about me as I was about them. Blackbirds and finches would perch themselves above me and red-breasted robins would sing their sweet songs. Meanwhile I would close my eyes and float into a reverie – sliding deep within my dreams wherein these creatures would take me welcomingly into their world. Soon, in these times of wonderment did I learn to speak with the birds and animals, and then did they become my true friends.

Now at this time our land was ruled over by King

Vortigern, who had usurped power following the death of King Constantine. Vortigern had seized the throne from Constantine's brothers Uther and Pendragon, who were forced to retreat to far-off realms. King Vortigern had learnt from those about him that I was a 'child of the Devil' – the illegitimate offspring of a convent nun – and that I did appear to harbour within my heart and soul strange powers that were not of this world. And so it came to pass one day, soon after my fifth birthday, that my mother and I were summoned unto the King's Court, and the King did begin to question my mother at length about my strange conception.

'Upon his soul and mine, my lord King, never have I known the man who impregnated me,' she did reply with an anguished voice. 'I know only one thing. I was resting in my chamber, and there appeared to me a most handsome young priest. He urged me not to be afraid and began speaking with me in a friendly and comforting way. However he then took me in his arms and began to kiss me on the mouth. Then he made love to me and made me pregnant. And when I awoke in the morning he had gone. No-one knew who he was or whence he came. A monk in my village told me I had been with the Devil...'

Now did King Vortigern turn to one of his most trusted, elderly advisors and asked if such a spirit-visitation could indeed be possible. And the wise and learned man hath replied: 'I have read in the books of

our philosophers and in numerous histories that many men have been conceived in this way. As Apuleius maintained, concerning the god of Socrates, there are between the earth and the moon certain spirits whom we call incubi. They have elements of both human and angelic nature and, when it pleases them, they assume human form and have relations with women...'

Perplexed and still unsure concerning these affairs, King Vortigern hath now turned his gaze to me. Full well do I remember his lined and wrinkled skin, the menace in his eyes, and his gruff, unfriendly voice.

'So you are the devil-child, young Merlin Ambrosius,' he sayeth, a sneer upon his lips.

'By what means have you acquired your magickal soul – are you in truth the offspring of an incubus? For then indeed shall we make claim to test your mystic powers...'

Yet was I too young in years to gauge the nature of his question but I did feel within myself the challenge in his words, and I knew full well that the magick in my soul would now be put unto the test.

King Vortigern now did tell me of the great fortress he was building on Salisbury Plain, for to keep back any threat from the hostile armies of Uther and Pendragon. And yet was he was deeply puzzled for, even though the walls had indeed been fashioned strong and true from thick and sturdy stone, each time the fortress did near completion, then during the night would a rumbling

force erupt from beneath the ground, shattering the walls and causing the fortress to crumble into ruins. And as he spoke I did half-close my eyes, falling once again into a reverie. A swirling mist now arose from all quarters, and a strange and wondrous vision did come before me:

I saw two mighty and fearful dragons – one red, the other white – writhing beneath the ground, locked in what seemed to me to be a never-ending combat. Flames did blaze forth from their nostrils as the dragons engaged each other in their deadly contest, shaking the earth around them – and wreaking havoc upon the troubled fortress above.

And this struggle of the warring dragons brought yet another portent: For I was warned in my vision that the death of the red dragon would portend the death of King Vortigern himself. Then did I convey the import of these omens as well as I was able, for I was still young in the ways of magick and prophecy, and yet the King was loathe to heed my truth. For though he was troubled by my words, chose he not to heed my warnings.

Later hath the King's followers escorted me back unto the village with my mother. And on our arrival there I did overhear the courtiers urging good priest Blaise to do whatever he might to banish the demons from my

soul. But soon I heard as well that my prophecy had indeed come to pass. For Uther and his brother Pendragon did land in Britain with a new army and did with ease overcome the forces of King Vortigern. And the King himself hath burnt to death, his fortress on Salisbury Plain engulfed by flames, and Uther and his brother did then become joint sovereigns of our land.

Several years later, while I was yet still a young man, Uther and Pendragon took themselves to war against Hengist, leader of the Saxon invaders. And I knew that tragedy would befall one of our Kings. For in my dream I saw two ravens – one clutching a feather in its beak and the other pierced through its heart by a bloody arrow. Pendragon fell in battle, mortally wounded by an attacker, but Uther did rally his forces and claim a mighty victory. And he was able still to rule, taking the name Pendragon to honour his dead brother.

...the dragons engaged each other in their deadly contest...

THE CALL OF THE
FOREST

ome years later did I take myself away to live alone within the forest. My mother was much aggrieved when I told her I was departing and she then took me within her arms, weeping and imploring me to stay. But I knew full well that she now found her peace and solace within the bosom of the Church, whilst a different calling had arisen in my heart. For I was drawn instead to the wild places, to realms where others seldom ventured. As long as I could remember, I would listen to the murmurings at night of the venturesome and restless wind, and in the spirit-vision of my soul would I then rise high into the dark and brooding sky, dancing with the sylphs, sprites and faeries of the Nightland. I rejoiced too in the songs of wild ravens, in the crashing of thunder and lightning, and in the bubbling laughter of fast-flowing rivers. And I loved to listen to the rustling of leaves – especially the leaves of the mighty oak, ash and birch – for legends of the Ancient Ones were whispered here, and I took pleasure indeed in the cautious peerings of the forest animals who often showed themselves at dusk, anxious

to determine whether I was friend or foe. In truth I knew I could find my sustenance within the forest, for I could hunt deer, trap lazy dappled fish in the quieter streams, and feed upon the wild fruits and berries that grew abundantly in the untamed valleys. The forest would be my home for evermore – I knew this in my heart – and henceforth I sought to live alone. I found a secluded cave for my shelter, with a clearwater stream but a few paces away, collected what few personal possessions had accrued to me during my years in the village, and took myself off into the forest for what I thought within my heart would now be a life of solitary retreat.

In the ensuing months and years I did become one with the forest and as wild as all that surrounded me: I let my hair fall in long, flowing folds upon my shoulders and allowed bristles to flourish upon my cheeks and on my chin like gorse upon the moor. I did drape across my back the skins of animals whom I had slain in the hunt, but you must know – for it is a truth I needs must share – that I never slew an animal in anger, nor killed any living creature for sport or whimsy. And always did I give my thanks and blessings to those animals who had surrendered themselves to me in the hunt. Some of these creatures I also took within my deepest self – as spirit-helpers and animals of power. Henceforth they would nestle in my soul, speak to me in my dreams, and accompany me in the ways of magick.

The forest would be my home for evermore...

It was in the early hours of sunrise or in the ebbing hours of dusk in the forest glades and thickets, beside the fast flowing streams and in the forgotten valleys, that my instructors in magick first came to me from the Otherworld. Oft have I been with the Horned One, who is called Finn or Cernunnos – Lord of Animals. Many times have I drunk his mead, danced with him in wild revelry and sung the songs of his spirit-helpers. For the Lord of Animals is mighty in his magick power and hath many creatures within his domain – the wily badger, raging boar, wise otter, ever-watchful eagle and nimble deer, and yet many more besides. The mighty Lord of Animals hath appeared before me, draped in furs and feathers – with wild serpents around his neck, and noble antlers for his crown. I have seen the wild wolf lie down beside him, and watched the raging bull humbly submit before his gaze. I have heard him sing the song of the raven and share the secrets of the owl. And he hath taught me to dance the songs of Earth, Air, Fire and Water, and to become one with the Mighty Stag, taking within me its noble strength and courage. And the Lord of Animals hath taught me too to change my form – losing my shape within the embers of a fire, within the flowing waters of a stream, in the wisps of a cloud or midst the pebbles of the earth. Oft have I danced like a wild beast, becoming like unto its nature, becoming one

In the ensuing months I did become one with the forest...

with its spirit. So too have I donned the Stag's antler crown, clothed myself in furs, and danced the dance of the First Day – when all was yet young and the wars of hostile invaders had not yet come upon our land.

So too have I met with the Fair Lady of the Flowers, who hath instructed me in the magick scents of plants – for to take me to the wondrous land beyond the Veil of Mist, and who hath revealed to me the soft tenderness of love and caring. For I have tasted her sweet kiss, caressed her smooth skin, and have lost myself within the sweet tangle of her long and flowing hair. And she hath nurtured me at her breast, fed me with her songs, and breathed into me the joy of life – for it is she who hath brought all things to be and who makes all things grow and prosper in the light of day. And she too hath rejoiced with the Lord of Animals and danced in the meadows of the Sun.

But I have seen her other face – the face of Morrigan the Dark, who hath both terror and death within her soul. And she hath led me down midst certain sacred rocks, to a path which leads unto the Veil of Mist which divides the worlds of the living and dying, and she hath revealed to me realms that few in this world could ever know. Where live incubi and succubi who possess the souls of the living as they slumber, and also the spirits of

I met with the Fair Lady of the Flowers...

death and decay who venture forth and bring upon us plagues and vermin. Where dwell the Angry Ones who vent their rage in winter hail-storms and vengeful demons who pour the venom of hatred into the souls of jealous men. These things have I seen.

But the Fair Lady of Flowers hath shown me too that all things have their coming into being, their fullness and their death, and she hath shown me these mysteries within her very form.

For I have seen her as a sweet and innocent child, a creature of the rainbow, yet changing then into a young, seductive woman – ensnaring her lovers with her wily charms and furtive promises. Then hath she also come before me as a mother of children and still further as an aged crone and hag – toothless and wrinkled like old and twisted leather. For she hath seen both beauty and despair, tenderness and fear, mellowness and decay. And she is all things, for she is the Goddess of the Earth and cyclic Moon.

These things have I learnt within the secret woods and valleys, in the hidden places that lie far from human gaze. And I have sought not the company of others, for all things have come to me from within the depths of the forest, beside the sacred flowing stream or in the quiet reverie of the cave – whence the Lord of Animals or the Fair Lady of Flowers have come before me and instructed me in their ways.

Soon a dishevelled courtier came fully into view...

Many waxings and wanings of the Moon did I spend in this way, alone and yet enriched. And yet, in time was it shown to me that though I had taken leave of humanfolk, they had not taken leave of me. One day, many years hence after departing my mother's village, I heard human tramplings in the forest — the scurrying of small animals, the crashing of branches broken in haste and the crunching sound of fallen leaves trampled underfoot. And then someone calling my name — Mer...lin, Mer...lin...

Soon a dishevelled courtier came fully into view, his garments torn and stained by brambles, thorns and berries. And then, his trusty steed — drawn dutifully on a lead. Both were tired and worn by the ardour of their journey. 'Oh, Merlin,' the courtier cried out when he saw me, 'I have looked for you many long days, for King Uther would have you come unto his Court. He seeks counsel with you, for he knows your ways in magick and prophecy, and he would have you come before him, just as you once gave oracles before King Vortigern.'

For my part, though, I felt no bond within my heart — either with Kings or with commonfolk — and no need to tarry at their beck and call. Perhaps there was yet a certain pride within my soul, a feeling bred of knowing that this forest was my true domain and sanctuary, that I alone held sway in these woods and would not be

summoned forth against my will. For a time, then, I kept my silence, pondering the request, before finally offering a response:

'I am willing to give counsel to the King but I shall not come at his beckoning to his Court, for I am not his servant... I serve only those Sacred and Ancient Ones whose power and wisdom uplifts us all. And if it pleaseth you, do advise the King that needs be he must instead come here, alone – for this forest where I dwell is now my place of sacred magick, and this is the realm where mysteries are revealed.'

On hearing this, the courtier began to protest and argue and gesture in the air, knowing full well that the King would be mightily displeased by my response to his request. For myself, I saw no fear in that. ' This is my reply to the King...,' I did say with bold resolve, withdrawing then unto the shadows of the forest. ' I will await his presence here...'

It is said that when the courtier returned to King Uther's court and advised him thus, that he flew into a raging temper and could not for a time be calmed – for no subject in the land would dare impose terms upon the bidding of the King. But then, as he did with time come to understand that in these matters I, Merlin, held power and not he, King Uther did agree to make the solitary journey into the forest. I saw, though, that in truth he only made the final steps alone – for he was a proud monarch intent on holding unto himself the

respect of all around him. And so it came to pass that the King did come unto my realm with trusted members of his court – a regal gathering of knights and other men on horseback. And then did the King take instructions from a loyal courtier at the edge of the forest, and venture forth into the forest by himself.

And so it was that I saw him coming – long ere his approach – and decided then to greet him first not as Merlin the sage and wise counsellor, but in the form of a deformed and humble shepherd who could perhaps offer guidance midst the twisting pathways of the forest.

So then King Uther espied me in a forest glade, as I stood attending a few of my straggler sheep. And he could tell from my hunched and twisted form that the trials of many wintery seasons had taken their toll upon my body, that I was well and truly bent over by the years. 'Good shepherd,' exhorted the King, feigning humility and a politeness in his manner, '... I am new to these lands and would urge your counsel – please tell me where the wise and noble Merlin dwells, and if you have already made his acquaintance and know his whereabouts, please take me to him – a gold sovereign will be your reward...'

Relief fell upon the King's anxious brow as I looked up from my rags and straggler sheep and sought to answer in my aged and croaking voice. A sense of wonderment, too, that a humble shepherd could somehow know in truth who came before him...: 'Oh yes, my noble King –

I do indeed know the whereabouts of the wise and fabled Merlin, and I will guide you to his cave...'

But then, before the King had time to ponder on these mysteries, I performed my magick in an instant before him. Turning full circle within the blinking of an eye, and with secret intonings to the Ancient Ones, did I cast away my humble shepherd's vestments and conjure myself instead into the form of a handsome and well groomed young man – a valiant prince within the wilderness.

King Uther was amazed – nay, dumbstruck – and a rapt silence fell upon him as he gathered unto him his thoughts, for he could hardly believe what he had just witnessed. But then he saw in truth who I was: 'Ah, Merlin – you are indeed a master of magickal disguises – and I know now that it is you...'

Drawing deep a sigh of apt relief the King did relax his guard and now began to speak more freely: 'I am truly glad to have found you, for I urgently seek your counsel in the ways of magick and enchantment. For I have great need of your special guidance in a matter that hath seized my heart...'

Not knowing the King's intent, yet respectful of his honour, I now bade him continue. The King meantime took me by the arm, speaking in soft and muted tones as we walked into a sunlit glade.

'I have been in recent times with Gorlois, Duke of Cornwall, whose fortress at Tintagel stands proud and

mighty on our western shores. And yet it is not with him so much as with his wife – the fair and beautiful Yguerne – that this tale rests, for I have fallen deep in love with her, and I know not where to turn.

'For I see her precious, wondrous face in my reveries each night – I look deep within the crystal pools which are her eyes and find my own love resounding in her soul. I sense her gentle breath upon my cheek as we embrace, and I know we are in truth one spirit... and yet Yguerne is with another, a man who cannot know the depths of love I feel and yearn for.

'But all of this is yet to no avail, for Yguerne resists the call to meet me in the bonding of this love. And whilst I sojourned in Carduel, close by to Tintagel Fortress, then did I meet with Gorlois and fair Yguerne, and whilst paying him due respect, made it known through a secret message to Yguerne that I sought her private counsel – alone, in relation to matters of the heart. My own councillor, Ulfin, who is beyond reproach and loyal to the death, hath passed this message to Yguerne by his own hand, but she hath resisted all further efforts on my part to meet with me, and I fear my love may be in vain.

'Further, I have heard tell that Yguerne hath told Gorlois of my amorous advances and he hath hidden his wife within a tower at Tintagel until my passions cool. Tell me, Merlin – wise and trusted sage – in what manner your magick may yet come to my aid in this affair...'

Yguerne resists the call to meet me
in the bonding of this love...

In truth, the King's account took me by surprise and it was some time before I could share with him my answer. But then a path of action laid itself before me, and I proposed it to the King.

'What say you to a plan whereby I take you to her heart through a disguise?' I asked him. Venturing further, I now told him of a magick spell – a secret formula wondrous and powerful in its working – which could needs be transform his appearance into the very form of Lord Gorlois himself.

And so it came to pass that I conjured my magick on the evening of the waxing moon, which doth allow for all things to reach their fullness and prosperity. Through my potent spell, King Uther now took unto himself the form of Duke Gorlois, whilst loyal Ulfin hath become in all manner of appearances the Duke's trusted companion. For myself, I posed as Britaelis, a Cornishman well known and liked by all at Tintagel.

Together we journeyed westwards to Tintagel and, through our authority with the guards, sought out the fortress wherein Gorlois had secreted his wife from view. In such a way was King Uther welcomed at the castle by Yguerne, who had no suspicions in her heart and took unto her bed that night a man whom she thought in truth to be her husband. And so it came to pass that on this special evening of love-making and deep disguise, that the child later known as Arthur was conceived and brought into this world.

After this regal sojourn in magick – a venture which, dare I confess it, brought both warmth and mischief to my heart – I did return unto the forest. But fate took then yet another turn, for word reached me soon afterwards from King Uther's court that Duke Gorlois had been slain in battle – in this way opening forth an honest path to Yguerne's charms and graces. And so it was that in due course King Uther was able to win the heart of fair Yguerne and make her his Queen.

When the babe called Arthur was born it was thought by most that he in truth was Duke Gorlois' son, though the King and I knew otherwise. Trusting me with his secret, King Uther urged me to be a guardian for the boy and bring him up myself, as if I were his father. But clearly this could not be, for my ways in the forest were no place for a young infant.

Instead a means was found for Arthur to become the charge of Sir Hector, a loyal knight indeed, who had his own young son, named Kay. Henceforth Arthur and Kay would grow up as brothers, young Arthur not knowing that royal blood ran in his veins.

THE BUILDING OF THE ROUND TABLE AT CAMELOT

everal years passed and the ways of King Uther and his nobles were now far distant from my mind. But then word came to me through Ulfin – who sought me out in the depths of the forest and did implore me to come in haste unto King Uther's court. For there was a matter of great import to discuss and, needs be, my presence at the court was demanded.

With a smile within my heart, for I knew this time I must surely grace the King rather than have him visit me, I did venture forth from the forest with Ulfin, and ride with him on his steed to Uther's castle.

King Uther greeted me at court, his arms outstretched arms ere I had been his long departed son – which pleased me mightily indeed. We then withdrew unto a private chamber to talk of matters dear within his heart.

Drawing me to his side, which he was wont to do when he spoke with hushed voice, King Uther said he sought to gather round him in his castle a group of valiant and

I did venture forth from the forest with Ulfin...

trusted knights, pledged to his command, who held amongst themselves all that was true and bold and worthy in the land. Further, that these worthy knights would in due time assemble in a large hall within the castle and take their places, one by one, at a large round table – 'round in the likeness of the world' as he would have it – and so constructed that all men would have an equal place, and none should consider himself in higher favour than another. King Uther sought places here for thrice fifty valiant knights, and wished that their names should be emblazoned in golden letters upon each chair.

The King now fixed his eyes firm upon me, and with his hand upon my shoulder asked how I should conjure such artistry as this to honour him – a wondrous table that would seat the noblest warriors in the kingdom... Indeed, the King well knew that this was no human task – that in some way unbeknownst to him but well considered nonetheless, this marvellous creation would be wrought through magick, rather than by merely human hands.

I did assure the King that I had both the means and will required, that this fine table would soon be his to grace the Hall of Knights at his command. And yet I asked for seven days, for my magick once again demanded the waxing of the moon and the summoning of certain spirits for the task. Then, taking leave, I wished him well and made my way once more unto the forest whence I came.

On the evening of the next full moon...

There did I seek the very finest piece of oak that I could find – from a sturdy branch new-fallen through its natural weight to ground, as if intended for this purpose so to serve. Then taking my athame for a blade, and intoning calls to the spirits of the earth and sky – for the Mighty Oak is both of this world and the next – I did begin to fashion by my own hand a small round table that could fit within my palm. Upon this small but wondrous form did I apply the names of all the serving spirits at my command, and many more besides – for it is the magick of the Ancient Ones that doth sustain a purpose such as this. Then, too, did I make by my own hand in turn a small but precious chair to rest beside the table – carved in every detail fine, as I required.

Untutored men know not that like begetteth like, but this is surely at the very heart of magick. And so, with these small yet finely fashioned objects in my grasp – yet secreted from view – I did return to King Uther's court, and to the Hall of Knights wherein the Round Table would be housed to honour him.

On the evening of the next full moon – which all who practise magick know doth abundance bring – I evoked my helper-spirits thrice, and also called upon the Gods beyond the Veil of Mist, for such was the worthy nature of the King's intent – to seat around the Table of the World a hand-picked gathering of true and trusted knights. Then, before my eyes, and wondrous true, did one chair beget another, and the Round Table from

within my palm did yield itself to form. And when each object in its fullness had emerged, only then and with my magick calls resolved did the summoned Gods and spirits take their leave, allowing me to ponder on their work.

No common man hath glimpsed such mysteries in this world, for who this magick would believe? And yet within the blinking of an eye, there stood before me in King Uther's hall a wondrous and majestic round of oak — a table unmatched by any other in the land. And at equal intervals around its rim, thrice fifty oaken seats, each with fine engravings and heraldic crests assigned. I say thrice fifty but in truth two seats remained unnamed, for these would be assigned to knights as yet unknown — whose quest as knights would be to seek the Holy Grail.

With this fine conjuring in oak King Uther was well pleased, for here was majesty unequalled in the land — and room indeed for all the knights to take their place in homage to their King.

Once more I took my leave, departing Uther's court in the early hours of dawn. Yet not a year had passed before I once again was called — by Ulfin, who now had news of sadness to relay. For the King had died, but yet was without an heir — and a new and worthy monarch must be chosen for the realm. Uther's noblemen now called me to their side and sought my counsel and my trust, for they knew in truth that I would serve the Kingdom well.

Still I knew within my heart who would henceforth be our King, yet could I not spread this word abroad, for fear of breaking faith with Uther's wish. Instead I did resolve to set a task wherein only one could triumph — the true and undisputed heir within the land.

And so it came to pass in London town, that at Saint Stephen's Church on Christmas Day a strange sight did greet all those who came forth from Christian Mass. For in the cobbled yard outside the church now stood a wondrous rock — and none knew indeed who had brought it here, nor whence it came. Upon this rock there stood in turn an anvil, fashioned true from sturdy iron. And mounted strong within this anvil, embedded deep for all to see, there was a mighty sword with jewelled hilt — and these few words inscribed upon it thus: 'None but the man who may draw forth this sword should dare to take King Uther's throne.'

As crowds began to come and marvel round the rock, I issued then a challenge — that he who would be King should now come forth to claim his crown.

Many knights there were in Uther's realm, and all tried in turn to wrench the sword forth from its iron mount. And yet each had to turn away — not equal to the task. Many months then passed, and still there was no heir to take the throne.

But then there came to London town Sir Hector with his son Sir Kay, and with him too his foster-son, young Arthur — scarce fifteen years of age. Sir Kay had come

Arthur drew his sword with ease...

to take his place within a tournament of knights yet lacked a strong and trusty sword, for his was accidentally locked away and left behind. And so it came to pass that Arthur, with his brother's quest at hand, sought hard to find a sword for him that day. Now Arthur had heard tell of that fine marvel in the churchyard, for men talked often of the sword within the stone – yet he knew not the contest it entailed. So, boldly coming forward, Arthur drew the sword with ease – not knowing what this meant – and gave it gladly to Sir Kay, a welcome sword for him to use. But Sir Hector saw this too, and bid young Arthur tell him true whence it came.

And so it was that Sir Hector took the boy aside and had him press the sword once more into its mount, so all men gathered there were sure it was once more entrapped in stone. And some did try their hand again to draw the sword, in case the crown be theirs – but this to no avail.

Then silence fell upon the crowd again, as Arthur drew the sword forth from the rock. And all who stood and marvelled at this wonder knew that Arthur must be King. A mighty song of praise now rose up high into the sky, and all those gathered there now knew him as the leader of their land.

Yet Arthur was a youth, and one whose regal path was much in need of counsel and the guiding hand of others many years his elder in this world. In this I played my role, no doubt, for I was always by his side at times of

Arthur, in his courtly travels far and wide,
did fall in love with Guinevere...

great debate, and laid before him plans and grand designs for Camelot, his noble court and palace which we did build in Winchester forthwith. For here were regal towers and ramparts rising high above the fields. Within the fortress, magick fountains – with their waters healing pure – and wondrous plants whose scent was yet like nectar to the soul. Fair peacocks roamed the gardens, white lilies graced the ponds, and the streams around the castle flowed brim-full with orange carp. And all did agree that the Gods now smiled upon Camelot, for peace had come at last unto this land.

But also did I fashion for the King a fine and handsome coat of armour, which yet no sword nor spear could ever pierce. And in his private chamber, as a special gift from Merlin to his King, was a wise and mystic mirror wherein whatever one would wish to see would then appear. In such a way could Arthur travel far within his kingdom and of everything enquire, for his spirit now had eyes to see beyond the castle walls.

In time did it come to pass that a King must needs be find his Queen and Arthur, in his courtly travels far and wide, did fall in love with Guinevere – the fair and gracious daughter of King Leodegraunce. And Arthur hath fought a fierce and bloody war in Brittany to show before the court that he would be the bravest and most splendid King in all the world. And so it was that Arthur did wed his bride at Pentecost and bring her thence to Camelot for a feast of pomp and splendour at his court.

And soon afterwards King Uther's wish would also come to pass, for Arthur did decree that a mighty hall be built wherein the Round Table would now rest in splendour, so that all the valiant knights might take their place in honour of the realm. And when the time was nigh, I did summon each and every one of these worthy knights in turn around the circle oak, and called their name forth, and placed their crests above them on the wall. And then, before those gathered there, the King did unveil twelve statues of enemy lords slain by him in battle. And much feasting followed, and good cheer, for all at Camelot were of one accord.

But now was it also time to counsel each and every knight upon their quest. And thus I spake, to bind each knight to what was dear, and also to reveal a purpose strong and firm that they must hold within their hearts: that now their quest was for the Holy Grail – the sacred Cup of Truth which by the Ancient Ones was blessed. And above one empty seat have I placed the golden letters 'Siege Perilous'. And above the other empty seat no name hath yet been placed – for this seat will be filled by a knight of grace and virtue who will see the Grail.

When this was done I did take my leave from Camelot. And travelling then awhile to find my peace did I come once more to Brittany. Yet peace was not to be my friend nor my comforter in sleep. For the Gods do move amidst the ways of men, and our lives do take strange twists and turns upon this Earth.

My Love for Vivian

And so now must I tell you of fair Vivian, for she is the lover who attends my dreams at night and who hath entranced me with her coy and magick ways. And as I resideth here in Brittany within this magic tower and do pen this chronicle forthwith to tell my tale, even now does great love rise up within my heart for her, though I fear I may be snared within her spell for all eternity.

It came to pass that I should see her first at that most lovely place of all – the Fount of Barenton – which is a sanctuary indeed, and a haven for the soul. For oft have I come to Brittany and thence unto the forest of Paimpont-Broceliande. And there lies within a clearing in that vast forest the most hallowed land of all, wherein, as I heard tell, some do come to cure their madness in the healing waters of the fount. For am I mad, or have I been, or was it always thus ? In truth I do not know, for the Gods fill my dreams with awe, and have haunted me for all my days and years upon this earth.

Barenton, from ancient times, hath been a mystic place – for here it is that Belenos, the God of Sun, hath long

...she was young and gentle too,

with a breath of roses on her cheek...

been honoured ages past. And to this place, indeed, there came a Goddess of the Sun – or so I thought – for here did I espy the wondrous Vivian as she took water from the fount.

And she was young and gentle too, with a breath of roses on her cheek, and her eyes were deep like pearls of dew upon a leaf. But I was aged and worn with wrinkles on my brow, and with a hoary beard and weathered skin looked not fit for any save those hags who rage and rant on Hallow's Eve.

Yet did I love her from that moment, and my magick must perform before her now. And so it was I conjured all my changes to effect, and did appear before fair Vivian as a charming youth indeed, and not as one to fright a graceful maiden half to death. Now could I be handsome too – and also much admired – a traveller to these parts who yet knew courts of Kings and Queens and doth have much to tell. And Vivian saw this handsome man – not me – and through his charm was drawn to make brief talk in welcoming exchange.

Now did she question me and I was quick to tell a tale: I am a wandering manservant from the courts of distant lands and have come to meet my master in this place. And many trades and skills have I engaged to serve the Kings and Queens and Dukes who bid me thus from many realms...

But then a question formed upon her lips: 'For tell me, sir, some more about your trades...' And when at

first I did not meet her gaze, she asked again a second time, and waited so to hear. And so I told her thus, for fancy took my thoughts this day:

'Sometimes through magick arts of old have I lifted castles high within the air, to rid the Kings and Queens of fierce attack and save their men from death and bloodshed on the ground. Or else have I myself made rivers form and writhe like snakes upon the earth, and walked upon the lapping waters of a lake without so much as have my feet be wet whilst venturing ashore...'

Fair Vivian now knew that magick was abroad and grew alarmed, for clearly I was not whom I should seem to be within that handsome guise. And so she quizzed me further on the magick arts and charms that lay within my grasp. Yet was I loathe to show her further who I was, and whence these mysteries came within my ken. But she hath taken me aside and put her sweet hand upon my own, and looked entreatingly indeed within my eyes:

'What magick, sir, is this... please show me more...'

And so, in a blinking of an eye, and with potent magick at my call did I beat my wooden staff upon the fount. And then before her very eyes did spring a cavalcade of dancing knights and ladies fair. And within their midst a fine and wondrous castle did appear, its turrets rising high into the air. But then these fine and handsome knights and ladies did take themselves away within the castle gate, passing swift across

the moat in double file, to hide themselves from view.

This hath brought joy and laughter to fair Vivian, and entreatingly hath she hugged me close and begged me tell and show her more. And for myself, I have felt the warming fires of love rise up within me, and I would bed her on the ferny banks of Broceliande. But yet she teaseth me, and maketh sweet talk, but would not my amorous intent engage. Nor would she have me take her maidenhead that day.

But Vivian doth have my heart within her clasp and I have shown her other marvels of the mystic arts. For before her very gaze have I summoned forth an orchard full with burnished trees and ripe fruits and berries, and with speckled birds of song. And she hath seized these fruits in wonderment and tasted them as well, as if to test me true.

Yet then she hath departeth, for her father did await her swift return that day, and the hour was running late towards the eve. And many further days have I wandered in the leafy glades of Broceliande, awaiting her return.

Some days hence did she again appear, once more to take the waters of the fount. And this time, again hath she enquired of magick and my mystic ways – and how may I teach her in these arts of old. For my part, though, my heart still burned with flames of love and for a time the ways of magick were far distant from my thoughts. I sought to have this maiden for to love amidst the flowers and scented grasses of the glade.

Then, yet sensing my desires, hath she asked these things of me: 'Wise Merlin, my dear and lovely friend, do teach me this – how may I make a man fall fast asleep forever, and not wake till I ordain that it should come to pass?' But I knew this for a trick, and would not tell her of my charms and spells.

For seven days and nights hath fair Vivian stayed with me, despite her father's call, yet hath she not granted me her maidenhead in love. And still she begged me dear to share this magick spell with her.

When I refused this still, she then did say: 'In such a case, what magick would you conjure fair to put a woman so to sleep, that you might love her through the night and wake her in the morn?'

And like a fool who even knows the follies of his ways, have I granted her this spell. For Vivian, with her cunning thus concealed, hath written this upon a leaf of parchment – these conjurings of power – and then hath run off teasingly, and with great merriment, into the glade.

Still not have I engaged with her and tasted of her love, and then for five full days did she depart. But then she came again to Broceliande and called my name.

And now, again with pen and parchment in her hand, hath she coaxed me thus: 'If you will grant me just this spell I seek, will I indeed lie down with you in love and you may have my maidenhead amidst the flowers and trees and song...

'Pray tell me now how you would conjure into truth a tower upon a rocky crag, so high and strong and reaching for the clouds. Where I could take my lover so to keep unto myself within these walls. That at my very beck and call we could engage in love with fiery passions of the heart, and yet he could not leave that tower without my will?' And in my trust, perchance to gain her heart forthwith, have I revealed these spells and charms. And I have told fair Vivian of this potency and power...

And yet, what fool am I to share my magick thus? For she hath conjured strong and true and called my magick charms against me now. For of the eve, with waxing moon, hath she engaged the Gods of Old to call down all their force, this tower so to build. And taking hold of both my hands, hath she entreated me to come within. Then casting forth her robes before her feet, and free unto the night, hath she enticed me to her chamber midst the sweet and wondrous wafts of damask rose. And now have we enfolded one within the other upon her pillowed bed, and my spirit hath soared unto the heavens in sweet and wondrous bliss.

And yet am I a prisoner of my love, with eternity to grace. Fair Vivian doth visit with me here, both in the eve and also in the dawn of morning light, but then doth take herself away – her magic spells to conjure thus upon the world. And whilst her loving charms doth she bestow upon me still, for she hath captureth my soul,

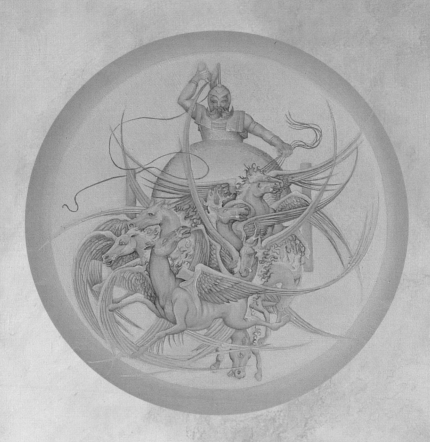

...she engaged the Gods of Old to call down all their force...

yet am I old and withered in my years. And I must sit alone amidst my dreams and reveries – my fate to ponder hour upon each hour into the night.

Yet life doth have its own rewards and blessings given. For much upon the path of magick have I received through grace and wisdom from Cernunnos, Lord of Animals, and from the Fair Lady of the Flowers, who hath opened me to love – these marvels to behold. And now, as is decreed, I take my pen in hand and have my parchment here, forthwith to tell my tale. For I would share this wonderment with you, lest all these ancient truths and mysteries are lost unto the whisperings of the wind.

MAGICKAL

KNOWLEDGE

bOW YOU YOURSELF
MAY BECOME A WIZARD
OR A WITCh

@

The way of magick is a calling – indeed, a way of being in this wondrous world. For some of us it doth arise within as naturally as a breath of wind doth caress the earth, welcoming us to rise up and fly. We know not whence this calling comes, for it is a mystery, but it is a beckoning to discover who we are and what we must do whilst indeed we roam this earth, seeking our true purpose.

Sometimes the magick will come to us within the night, unexpected and unbidden. During slumber our soul doth unite with the dark forms of evening yet seeks the softly glowing light that fills our dreams. Perchance at this time in the night a bird will come to visit – an owl or raven – and fly three times around us as we sleep. And yet, this bird of night is calling us to wake, to have vision within our dream. And then there comes a song – a song at first heard only faintly, yet ever gathering in strength, that seems now to speak to us, deep within our heart. This bird is calling us through song, and we know

The way of magick is a calling...

then that this music of enchantment is ours alone — a special song of meaning and power that doth enrich and guide us as we make our journey through life. And we must remember this song if it is given to us in a dream, and when rising in the morning each day henceforth, evoke that song within our hearts as our greeting to the new day.

And yet for others the bird of night may not come unbidden, nor yet any other guide or helper-spirit. For these other seekers in the ways of magick, a journey of the soul must henceforth be made to find the guides who will sustain and nurture us in this life. These guides will take us through the cracks between the worlds, into the deep valleys that lead towards the Veil of Mist, and to the company of the Ancient Ones who dance in the dawn of the First Day.

There is a tree, a mighty Sacred Oak, that yet is like a thousand oaks all conjured into one, and this tree riseth up unto the heavens — its branches reaching so high that they do disappear in the vastness beyond. And the roots of this mighty tree also reach way down into the earth, extending through the depths to the very base of the Lower Worlds. Through the branches and roots of this noble tree must we journey to find our helper-spirits — our guides, our magickal familiars — for without them our path will have no purpose, no intent, and we will wander aimless and alone.

Close now your eyes and summon unto your own

There is a tree, a mighty Sacred Oak,
that yet is a thousand oaks all conjured into one...

inner vision, the form and majesty of this mighty and awesome tree, this Sacred Oak of Ancient Mysteries. See now that at the base of this tree there swings open a large wooden door, above which is written your name. This door is calling you to enter, to explore the mysteries which lie within.

Now hold within your vision that you are passing through the doorway down into a dark and mysterious tunnel which burrows deep into the earth. And it may be that for the moment this tunnel seems dark and forbidding but in due time you feel the presence of the earth spirits around you – goblins, elves and playful Nature sprites – urging you on, supportive but unseen. As you move further along this tunnel you glimpse in the distance a faint light, and flickerings from this light play lightly upon the furrowed walls of the tunnel. The light now calls you towards it, calls you ever onwards, and you know that as you draw closer to its source soon will you enter another realm, a world where magick dwells and where sacred knowledge is bestowed. For this is surely the domain wherein helper-spirits may be found, the familiars of power, who will form a lasting bond in magick with you and will help you find your path within these mystic realms.

As you make your way yet further to the light, now do its beams fall free upon your face, enriching you with strength and bold resolve. And finally will you come to that point in the tunnel where it openeth forth to a

vastness beyond – for this is the boundless realm of magick and wonderment. Here too dwell the helper-guides of spirit.

Face now with arms outstretched towards the mystic light, and call forth for your magical ally – your helper-spirit – to come before you. And yet must this call come up from within your heart, not in words so much as through a yearning from the soul. And this call will go forth, like a rippling eddy within a mountain stream, to summon forth a spirit-being who will then come and serve you. Judge not in the first instance who this creature may be – do not expect grand winged horses, or striped wildcats, or gleaming, golden snakes. For perchance the spirit-being who will come before you will be a humble sparrow, a meek and timid badger, or a little field-mouse. Yet all of these are Nature's creatures, and all have their place in this world and the next. For the helper-being who doth appear before you hath been offered as a gift, and so should you receive it with grace in the spirit it is given. Indeed, this creature will surely dance around you, appearing to you from the North, South, East and West. Welcome it in your heart, speak with it through your soul, and make dance with it in the mystic light – rejoicing that the Lords and Goddesses of Nature have bestowed this gift upon you. Then, as you do embrace this creature deep within your heart, take it back with you down through the tunnel to the waking world whence you came. And your helper-guide

will be with you always, and will serve you in future times, when you venture yet again towards the mystic light. For this guide, and others too who may henceforth present themselves, will help you find your way midst the Gods and spirits of the Inner Worlds.

Now as you cometh with your magical ally through the tunnel, once more do you arrive at the wooden door which is found at the base of the mighty oak. Close it firm behind you, with respect for what hath been bestowed upon you. And as you stand there, taking deep within your heart this gift of knowledge from the Gods, and having made your first steps upon the magick path, then are two things required of you. The first is that you must now take a magickal name known to none other than yourself, and the second is that you make a private offering of thanks unto the Gods.

Your magick name will now cometh as one which sings to you from the depths within your soul, and which is indeed a symbol of your bond with the mystic Inner Worlds. For this name needs be must remain your most prized secret and must never be entrusted to another, for it doth hold your essence and your power. Stand now before the door of the Ancient Oak – the portal of mysteries – hold your hands up high unto the Heavens, and receive this magick name – it will well up within you and reveal itself in time. Then, in your own way, maketh a gift of thanks, an offering to the Gods of precious things from Nature which are offered back in grace.

These may be things which have a value dear unto your soul – a feather of great beauty, a jewelled pebble from a stream, a richly mottled leaf, or something fashioned by your own hand.

...so should we live our lives
according to the ways of the Ancient Ones...

The Mystic Festivals

@

Let me now tell you once again that the whole world floweth like a stream through the seasons, from one cycle unto the next, beneath the ever-watchful guidance of our Lady of the Moon. And so as surely as the time of harvesting crops doth follow from the sowing of the seed, so should we live our lives according to the ways of the Ancient Ones.

And amongst my people have we honoured the Ancient Ones thus, with festivals lit with great bonfires to the Heavens and accompanied by much merriment and song, but also with tales and legends told in quiet memory of those who have gone before us. Also have we held up our hands on high to call on Lugh, King of the Wind, or to salute Belenos, King of Flame. And we have drunk from the sacred well to greet Llyr, King of Water, and we have made our sacrifices to honour Cernunnos, King of Earth.

These, then, are our times of honour – our celebrations for the Ancient Ones:

Each new year upon this Earth shall have its start upon the first full moon of Scorpio's reign within the heavens, and this festival is called Samhain (* the last evening of October). For now are the Gates of

So too have we offered blessings for those who have
passed before us through the veil of mist...

Otherworld flung open and the shades of the dead have come amongst us. And many have gathered to tell the tales of old on wintery nights.

So too have we offered blessings for those who have passed before us through the Veil of Mist. By this time have we sown our seeds within the earth for good crops to grow, and we have stored our crops from the harvest which is past. We have gathered forth our cattle, and slain those beasts whose meat we need to give us strength and sustenance, and we have shared our provisions with the weary and needy – and with those in grief who mourn the newly dead.

And for an omen have some made marks upon certain gathered stones and have then hurled them far into the bonfire flames which light the heavens by night. And then, as dawn followeth the eve, have they henceforth sought the stones within the ashes of the fire – for to seek their special fortune as an omen in that place.

Also at this time have we sung our praises to Dagda, Lord of Life and Death, and to Morrigu, Great Queen of Phantoms and Demons, and also to the ancient departed ones who have gone before.

Then with the passing of the Moon shall we come unto Imbolc or Oimelc, which beginneth on the first full moon of Aquarius the Water-bearer (*the last evening of

January). At this time shall the lambs be born and the milk of ewes flow forth. And we shall pay our tributes then to the mighty Goddess Brighid who hath travelled far and wide upon this Earth bringing good fortune and happiness to every household in the land. Some folks in truth have spread ashes in their hearth to see where Brighid hath left her mark. And for those who have seen her footprints in the ashes, good tidings and great blessings will follow. And if she hath left a small mark or line within the ashes – so too to them will some good fortune come. But for those who did not see the sign, they must indeed make their offerings to Brighid at this time, to seek her favours and the goodness of her heart.

For Brighid hath breathed life into the dead, and brought great healing unto our people. And she hath given her blessings unto those womenfolk who do labour with the birth of their children. So too doth she light the fires of hope and vision in those who bring forth poems and fine music for our soul's delight. And now at Imbolc is it time for us to make our magick spells for to seek our destinies and knowledge of future happenings which shall come to pass.

Now cometh the first day of summer and the first full moon of Taurus, which is Bealtaine (*the last evening of April). And we have called forth praises to the Lord of

Animals and to the Fair Lady of the Flowers who bring great blessings to our lives.

From now until Samhain is the time of the Greater Sun, and shall it shine forth within our souls, for in truth Bealtaine means 'bright fire'. And we have raised up a mighty May-pole, true and fair, like a tree which riseth up into the sky, and we have lain upon it ribbons, flowers and bright coloured garlands. And all have gathered here about and danced a merry dance around the pole and sung their songs of joy long into the night. So too have we lain bright flowers and garlands upon the cattle grazing in the fields and we have tied rowan berries on the posts beside our doorways, and taken time into our hearts to think upon the nature of our strength and the truth of our desires. For at this time hath mighty Lugh, Lord of Light and King of the Sky, come forth to make his conquests in the world.

And now at last cometh the time of harvest, which is given to us by the great Lugh Lamhfada, who doth ride his white steed through the skies. For Lughnasadh - Lugh's celebration – doth come with the first full moon of Leo (*the last evening in July), and this is indeed a time to make our spells of good fortune and abundance. So too shall we honour the Goddess Macha, who is also called Tailtiu – who rideth forth to war but is also a Queen of Peace who doth give to all in times of need.

At Lughnasadh shall the tribes and their leaders come together and lay down their weapons and make their peace with games and songs and races in their horse-drawn chariots. And all of us shall be mindful at this time of our words given in trust, one to the other, for the times which lie ahead.

@

In truth, these four festivals of Samhain, Imbolc, Bealtaine and Lughnasadh do mark the passing of the year from season unto season, and we must honour the Ancient Ones who have gone before us in this world. For we have seen this in the sowing of the seed, and in the first blooms which come with the passing of the winter snow. And the hawthorn bush hath burst forth into flower, the birds of summer have flown across the skies, and oats have ripened in the field.

And so it hath come to pass, from the earliest times unto all ages henceforth, that one moon follows another, and night yields unto day. And with the coming of each sacred eve have we then burnt the holy fires long into the depths of the night, calling forth upon the Gods to share their tidings of good fortune amongst us.

So too have we ventured forth to make our sacred magick thus, and we have honoured the Ancient Ones and walked the mystic path like those who have gone before us.

THE FIVE ELEMENTS

SPIRIT

AIR

FIRE

WATER

EARTH

Whence this world arose and how it did come to be fashioned by the Old Gods – the Timeless Ones of the First Time – is a mystery that surely no human being can fathom. But this much is known – that in forming the language of Creation, these Gods did make use of five Elements. All things around us, all creatures who live and breathe, and all of the healing and nourishing plants, flowers and wild herbs, have been created with various degrees of Earth, Water, Fire and Air, and sustained through Spirit. In this way are all things and all beings made, for Spirit doth unite us all.

Through magick do we conjure the Elements, evoking unto us the special properties of the Life-force for our learning and our coming-into-light. And yet are there secret paths of knowledge that have fallen from the minds of men gripped with vanity and arrogance. For the way of Magick is a path to sacred knowledge, of reverence and humility – and the world is a wondrous place. Yet how many amongst us have fathomed these depths?

Spirit

In Spirit are all Mysteries revealed, yet who can speak of these sacred things? For Spirit lies beyond the Veil of Mist, beyond the Dance of the Ancient Ones, beyond the songs of the Old Gods – in the timeless Land of All Knowing.

SPIRIT IS YET AIR BUT NOT AIR

FIRE BUT NOT FIRE

WATER BUT NOT WATER

EARTH BUT NOT EARTH

SPIRIT IS THE SACRED, THE HALLOWED, THE PURE, THE
UNSPOKEN

SPIRIT IS BEING BEYOND FORM

SPIRIT UNITES US IN THE ISLES OF THE BLESSED

Within the magick circle, then is Spirit all around us: above, below, and in each of the Four Directions. No gem may be ascribed to Spirit, for it is a Mystery beyond Mysteries.

Air

Air is the Breath of Life, whom Father Sky hath breathed forth into us all. Air doth flow through all things – through the forests, hills and valleys, across the many seas of this world, and over lakes and barren land besides. Air giveth flight to birds, a shape to clouds, and

...in the sacred world of magick
are the mysteries kept safe and distant
from those who would profane them...

a home to thunder — and is the herald of changing times. For who hath not glimpsed shadows of the Gods dancing in the sunset or heard them summoning the storms at night?

Air maketh its home in the High Heavens and yet it doth flow freely, like a gift for all to share. Who has seen it come, yet who hath not felt its presence? For it moves amongst us like an unseen visitor, yet gives us life and strength to be. And Air carrieth the wishes of the Ancient Ones, for they flow down into our world like a great bounty. Air cometh into our hearts, bringing joy and wisdom and knowing to our souls.

And you should know that those who guard the realm of Air are sylphs — pure creatures of truth and beauty whose ways are not yet sullied by the earthy ways of humankind. For these beings are like unto jewels of light, their wings glistening as crystal butterflies in the first Dawn. We may see them in a dance of light upon a leaf or petal, perchance amidst the forest dells or in the hidden glades where few have ventured.

The magickal symbol of Air is the athame or dagger. This small magick knife shall bear a black wooden handle. And upon its hilt may be inscribed the names and symbols of the Lord of Animals and the Fair Lady of the Flowers — for in this way you honour them. As you make your magick conjurings within the Air, the athame calls down the Spirits into form. In this way shall the Ancient Ones come amongst you.

Within the magick circle, Air is of the East and its sacred ceremonial gems are the sapphire, blue topaz, azurite and lapis lazuli. The King of Air is Lugh.

Fire

Fire cometh from the Sun, our Father in the sky whose warmth and radiance uplifts us all. With each day Father Sun doth bring his shafts of light against the enshrouding night, banishing the forces of the dark realms and yielding hope unto the world.

As followers upon the magick path, we needs be must have a fire within us too – a fire of vision which bringeth in its wake wisdom strong and true. Like logs upon a fire in winter, with their sparks and vibrant flames reaching high unto the night-sky, so too may we be the body of this light, offering ourselves unto the Gods as servants of their mystery and wonderment. For when we too are carriers of this flame, so doth our light – like that of Father Sun – go forth into the world as a beacon of the wise, and our hearts henceforth are full of warmth.

Yet in the sacred world of magick are the Mysteries kept safe and distant from those who would profane them, and Fire hath its guardians too. No-one may come unto the inner realm of Fire lest he first earneth the loyalty and deep respect of these awesome and wondrous guardians, who could easily vanquish idle wanderers untrained in the paths of wisdom. And the guardian-

...who hath not glimpsed shadows of the Gods
dancing in the sunset...

beings of Fire are salamanders — strange creatures to
behold. For a salamander is like unto a lizard, yet hath
the body of a cat and wieldeth the tail of a serpent.
Talons too it hath upon the very tips of all its feet, and
bright stars emblazoned upon its skin. And this creature
loves the Fire — for it is nourished by it — yet is it so cold
within itself that it cannot be harmed by the flames
which lap around it. Salamanders do help the
blacksmith in his task of forging mighty swords and
armour, feeding strength into the flames to melt the
iron and have it yield unto the blacksmith's purpose.
And yet the salamander is a mighty and tenacious
defender of the Fire — for its teeth drip with poison and
are fearsome in every way. Only the strongest magick
may hold the salamander at bay — then shall it be a loyal
ally and not an enemy to bar us on our quest.

Now the magickal symbol of Fire is the mystic wand,
and it shall be cut within the forest from a straight and
sturdy branch of almond or hazel wood, or from some
other tree that beareth nuts. Cut this branch with a
single blow with a pruning knife or sickle before the
rising of the sun, at that time of year when the tree is
soon to burst forth into blossom — for at this time the
tree is pregnant with its life and power. And should it be
that almond or hazel trees do not abound in the region
where you dwell, a straight staff of oak may also suffice
as a magick wand.

You must surely know that the wand is a symbol of the male member – and, like a phallus bestowing sperms of life, must needs be honoured for its powers of regeneration. The magick wand, like the Great Horned God who proffers his seed to Mother Earth, bringeth every thing to life once more. In such a way doth the magus employ his wand to harness and send forth his mystic power, bringing the sweet song of Creation to the world about him.

Within the magick circle, Fire is of the South and its sacred ceremonial gems are citrine quartz, yellow topaz and amber. The King of Fire is Belenos.

Water

The waters of life do heal us and purify our being. Without rain from the Heavens, then would the plants which nourish us wither and die, and without uplifting waters of the Spirit that flow into our soul from the Ancient Ones, then surely would our bodies perish.

For our thoughts and feelings are like unto eddies and currents that are found within a mountain stream, and they do flow freely into the hearts and minds of those around us. And at certain times it may come to pass that a pool of water is silent, its surface hardly rippled by the wind, with beams of sunlight extending far into the depths below. At such a time doth a deep calm come upon us, and our thoughts are filled with peace and

...then doth a force build within the water,
catching everything up within its wake...

reassurance, and we may surely wish to share this peace with others.

Yet at other times, and who may know the day, then doth a force build within the Water, catching everything up within its wake. Like untamed ocean waves which toss and turn, like raging seas which hurl themselves upon the rocky coastline, Water doth bear our thoughts and feelings to the further shores – and it doth bring our love, and yet also our rage, unto the lives of others. Accordingly shall we take heed of the tides of feeling which do rise up within us and have them flow to positive effect, in this way so to comfort and enrich the lives of those we know who are dear to us.

Within the sacred world of magick there are Undines – nymphs of Water who do haunt that place between the outer waking world of sunlight and the realm of secret and unspoken things which doth dwell deep within us all. For the Undines do lure men with their musical enchantments, creating sweet, intoxicating melodies with their harps or singing pure, uplifting songs for all who venture near. In such a way are we drawn unto the depths of our awareness, travelling still further upon the mystic path which leadeth in turn towards the Spirit.

The magickal symbol of Water is the Cup and then shall it be fashioned from glass or silver. For the Cup is a receptacle – holding true within its form the fluids

which have been poured therein. We too are summoned forth as vessels for the sacred waters, taking deep within our hearts and souls the many-fold gifts bestowed upon us by the Ancient Ones.

Within the magick circle Water is of the West and its sacred ceremonial gems are the amethyst, pearl and moonstone. The King of Water is Llyr.

Earth

As well you know, Earth hath been bestowed upon us by the Gods as our domain – yet also shall we honour the world of trees, flowers, herbs, animals and other living beings, for these too are the gift of the Ancient Ones. And Earth doth give us form – for the Spirit hath entereth the dust. Earth feeds us with her bounty, with clothes provided for our back, and she hath given shelter for our hours of sleep. And who must we praise as custodians of this Earth? Surely must we offer praises to the mighty Lord of Animals, who is known amongst us as Cernunnos, and so also to the Fair Lady of Flowers who is his wife and lover, and Mother of all who have come into this World.

Yet shall we all remember in our hearts that Earth is the resting place of Spirit, and a sanctuary which we all must honour. For within her secret entrances, and guarded by the Hidden Ones, shall we find the first pathways back towards the Veil of Mist. And yet Earth is

In such a way are we drawn unto the depths of our awareness...

both of this world and the Otherworld, for she is host to all the other Elements besides: Air doth blow upon her face, Fire doth ignite within her belly and spew forth from her mountains, Water flows through her deep valleys, and Spirit marketh upon her skin the sacred pathways of our quest. Earth is our dwelling till we pass beyond into the secret glades of Otherworld, yet whilst we do live in human form then shall we honour and respect the Earth whence we come.

The protectors of the Earth are gnomes, who do roam freely in the dark caverns beneath our feet, guarding our quarries and our buried treasures, and making their home beneath the roots of the Mighty Oak and other blessed trees. From time to time, no doubt, these gnomes do make merry with the lives of humanfolk, having their ways in mischief and making jokes. For oftentimes do they frighten children with their ugly wrinkled faces, or use their small picks and shovels to move elsewhere the seeds which we have planted in the soil. And yet, for all their pranks and their mischief, are these gnomes good and virtuous within their natures, and offer gifts of kindness when hard times come upon our lives.

The magickal symbol of Earth is the Pentacle or Disc. Perfect round, and fashioned by your very hand from stone or wood, then must it fit within your palm and

bear the sacred magick name which hath been given to you by the Ancient Ones. On the side which beareth your magick name shall you make also a five-pointed star, for this, sayeth all, is the form of humankind, with arms and legs outstretched and head held high. And on the other face of the pentacle maketh the form of a six-pointed star, like unto two intersecting triangles — one facing up, the other down — for this surely is the symbol of All That Is.

Within the magick circle Earth is of the North and its sacred ceremonial gem is the garnet, in all of its four colours. And the King of Earth is Cernunnos.

AWARENESS IN MAGICK

@

Magick doth bring us back to life again and helps us find our place upon this Earth. Surely doth magick lay before us the deep and sacred purpose we have buried deep within our souls. Magick may yet take us on a journey to the realms beyond the Veil of Mist but so too may it bring great strength and wisdom to our daily life of toil. For then shall we come to hear with greater hearing, and see with greater vision, and taste with greater taste, and smell the scents of life which are all around us. And so too shall our touch yield more surely unto the pleasures and the pains which abound in this world.

Hearing

Our hearing doth attune us to all things which arise about us and is bestowed on us through Spirit. The Sacred Word of the Most Ancient One doth echo through the halls of Creation, sending its call to every leaf and flower, to every stone and mountain, to every human being and animal alike. The Sacred Name doth sustain all that exists, and surely must we develop ears to hear it. For in the most hallowed realms of all,

Magick doth bring us back to life again...

exquisite music — more beautiful than one can grasp —
doth fill the heavens and purify the worlds below.

Seeing

Our sight is precious dear unto us all and is bestowed
upon us through Fire. For as I have said, the Fire of
Father Sun doth give us light, and through light may we
see. Our sight reacheth out unto the world of Nature,
and then do we rejoice amidst the diverse forms of all
that comes before us. But sight also ariseth within
ourselves as inner vision, taking light and understanding
unto the depths within our soul.

Tasting

Our sense of taste doth enable us to share the very
essence of other things that arise within this world, and
this gift is bestowed on us through Water. For since our
first days of life, suckling at our mother's breast to take
her milk, surely since that time have we learned to find
our pleasure in the sensual delights of food and wine —
and also to taste love with a tender kiss. Through taste
cometh a merging — both of flavours and of feelings
alike.

Smell

Surely is our sense of smell bestowed on us through
Earth. For the sweet fragrance or noxious odour of that

which is brought before us doth tell us then in what manner is it made, and then shall we know forthwith whether we are drawn unto its sweet and alluring scent or repelled by its gross and loathsome odour. For we all have seen how hunting dogs do follow hard upon the scent left by their prey, but a lover followeth the scent of his passions too. And the most beautiful perfumes and incenses do surely take us unto Paradise.

Touch

Our sense of touch doth connect us with all living things and is bestowed upon us through Air. The Ancient Ones hath given us bodies so to feel but yet also do thoughts and emotions rage all around us. And like the breath of wind which doth pervade the world and grant us life, so also may the way we touch and feel grace our human lives upon this Earth. For it may be that we do caress each other with the gentle touch of fingers onto skin, or touch another person's soul through the gift of caring and being kind.

HOW WE THEN MAY COME TO KNOW THE ELEMENTS

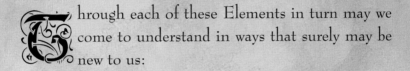

Through each of these Elements in turn may we come to understand in ways that surely may be new to us:

Through Spirit may we come to dwell upon the vastness of All That Is. And as we face unto the Heavens, our eyes closed and our arms uplifted, then may we dwell upon the infinite being which reacheth far beyond form, and the boundless wisdom of the Old Gods who hath created all things within the world as we know it. And then shall we surely give thanks for our life upon this earth, and take unto our hearts and souls this thought — that all living things are blessed and united through the Spirit of Creation. Then may we reflect indeed upon the wondrous mystery of our lives.

Through Air may we reflect upon the breath of the Most Ancient One – which doth sustain the Universe and give it life. Facing unto the East, our eyes closed and our soul embracing the realm of wonderment, shall we now fly unto the highest atmospheres and feel at one with the vibrant air which doth weave its currents through the mountains, oceans, valleys and human dwellings far below. Then shall we let our breath rise up and take its form in mighty winds and hurricanes and storms. And then shall calm descend, and surely will we see billowing clouds rise, and then dissolve from view. And then will we feel the ebb and flow within our breathing and take unto our hearts and souls the sacred Life-force which doth enrich our every day upon this earth.

Through Fire may we attune ourselves unto the flame which burns within our soul. Facing unto the South, our eyes closed and our soul embracing the realm of wonderment, we then may see our bodies sending forth to all quarters both light and life. Then shall we watch in awe as a glowing ember from our heart's radiance doth make its union with the flames that riseth from a log fire in the night, and then shall they both rise up unto the Heavens in a spirit of exultation. Now shall we gather our fire within us, nurturing the inner flame and hold dear the warmth which it doth yield unto our spirit.

For we know we may take this flame to any quarter we desire, and light our magick will to good effect.

Through Water may we come to know the deepest thoughts and feelings which do dwell within us all. Facing unto the West, our eyes closed and our soul embracing the realm of wonderment, do we then see ourselves tossed upon the waves of the First Sea – the wild and raging ocean from which all that may ever be doth come forth.

And then, as we do cast our thoughts within, then do we recall the tides of life which do sustain us – the blood which floweth full within our bodies and the pumping of our hearts inside our chests. And now shall we see ourselves become a crystal chalice, open unto the Heavens, and into which the waters of life are poured by the Ancient Ones.

Through Earth may we consider how we live and dwell within this world. Facing unto the North, our eyes closed and our soul embracing the realm of wonderment, then may we recall the certain things of life: our body which doth sustain the joys and toils of our travail, the food that feeds us, the ways of birth,

youth, maturity and aging – and the journey into dying. Then may we see ourselves becoming one within the rich brown earth, and dwelling once again within the trunk of the Sacred Oak. Or perchance like a Nature-sprite within the petals of a flower, or within the crystal beauty of a precious gemstone. For now may we become one within the Earth itself. And from our body doth sprout forth fruits and grains for harvest, and from our eyes cometh tears to water all the crops, and from our breast cometh milk to feed the living.

And so it is through magick that we do honour all the ways of knowing and feeling, for to take this wisdom deep within our soul. For with our mystic robes, our tools and magick aids, then do we respect the colours and affinities which are assigned unto the Gods and spirits, and through our chants and invocations which rend the Heavens, may we then call forth the Ancient Ones to dwell within our souls. And we have drunk from the sacred well and burnt sweet incense from the herbs and flowers to bring our greetings unto the Gods, and we have felt the touch of Spirit upon our skin and in our hearts.

WITHIN THE MAGICK CIRCLE

@

Oft have I made my magick callings in the depths of the forest night, summoning the Ancient Ones to come before me to work my spells or share with me their wisdom and their secrets. And now must I tell you more of this.

For you must find yourself a cleared space within the forest – far from idle human eyes and in a space where noble Oaks reach up high unto the heavens. So too, seek a place where flows a quickly moving stream, for here do the spirits of the glades rejoice.

Come unto this place donned in robes that are the colour of the earth and which are worn for this purpose alone, and wear about your waist a cord, for to have your magick blade close to hand. Bring with you too your magick wand and other mystic aids which do grace the magick quest, and which I shall describe forthwith.

Taking now your wooden wand within your hand, mark within the earth a circle that is some nine paces across, and within this furrow in the earth pour salt or chalk to mark its edge. And when the time cometh for making magick then shall you place a candle or a

Oft have I made my magick callings
in the depths of the forest night...

lantern at each of these points – East, South, West and North – for these are the Four Quarters. And maketh too a small altar and place it in the North within the circle – for here may you place your own implements of magick – your athame, your wand, your cup and your pentacle.

And just within the confines of the magick ring shall you place in the East a bowl of herbs and in due time light these herbs with a flame for to partake of their wondrous scent, for this is a symbol of Air. And in the South place a further lantern or a candle as a symbol of Fire. Thence too within the West a bowl of Water, and in the North a bowl of Earth. And if you wish it, you may also place a metal cauldron in the very centre of your ring – with herbs and gatherings of sacred wood to offer up, and flames of light and life to give good purpose. Then to have the magick circle come alive within your gaze shall you run and dance deosil (*clockwise) within the circle's rim, and point your magic blade tip-down towards the circle edge – and a ring of light shall then arise before you as you dance. And as you stamp your feet upon the earth, then shall the Gods and sprites take note that you have come amongst them.

But now take yourself unto the East within the circle rim and with your magick wand make the sign of the five-pointed star unto the sky .And thence unto all the other quarters – South, West and North in turn, before

returning to the Eastern quarter once again. Now, having lit the bowl of scented herbs which you have placed upon the ground, hold it high unto the Heavens and call the guardians this way: 'Lord of Air, I charge you with all the Power of the Ancient Ones to witness this rite and give protection to this realm...' And moving to the South and lifting up the lantern as a sacred light: 'Lord of Fire, I charge you with all the Power of the Ancient Ones to witness this rite and give protection to this realm...' And so to the Lord of Water in the West and thence unto the Lord of Earth in the North... and then close the circle in the East and give a blessing for the sealing of the rim. And in this way hath your magick circle become a sacred place within the grove of Oaks, and now may you make your magick purpose here, knowing full well – both within your mind and in your heart – that the Ancient Ones do now guard you true and strong upon your mystic quest.

And so it may be that you would summon Cernunnos, Lord of Animals, or mighty Lugh, The Shining One who rideth unto war upon his white steed. Or mighty Dagda, who is Lord of Life and Death. And so you take yourself unto the centre of your magick circle and call forth unto the heavens and hold these Ancient Guardians dear unto your heart and urge that they do appear before you on this sacred land that you have prepared with special herbs and sacred wood to grace their honour. And if you have offered unto them the

...all the spells of old will unfold themselves before you...

herbs which they do love, and if you have called their magick names, and intoned these names strong and true at the cycle of the Moon which is right for such callings, then will they come before you in that magick circle. And then in truth will you become one with them – for you have taken them into your very soul. In this way may you gain the sacred knowledge of the Ancient Ones for this knowledge is then within you, and all the secret lore and hidden things and spells of old will unfold themselves before you – in your visions and your dreams. And you will walk with the Gods and be like them in all your thoughts and actions, and in everything you do – from this time forth.

THE

MAGICK OF

ENCHANTMENT

CONCERNING THE
ALPHABET OF TREES

❧

Now must I tell you of the mystic Alphabet of Trees which hath been known by the bards since earliest times and which doth speak the language of prophecy and truth. Long hath it been the secret tongue of poets and of sages, for surely is it a language of enchantment that doth enrich and guide the soul. For through its lessons do the trees within the forest become like unto the Gods and spirits of an ancient land, and so too may we come to know the sacred language of the Earth.

For it came to pass when Elathan was King of all Ireland many years long past that this King had three sons, and one of these was Ogma. And Ogma was much skilled in the ways of the poets and he did conjure forth this Alphabet of the Trees as a language to be shared amongst those who know the sacred and mystic ways, and Ogma hath sent this wisdom forth amongst the bards of this and other lands. For until the time of Ogma were no poems or verses or wise fables ever written down in script, but yet were passed from mouth to ear amongst those who did know of these things. And Ogma hath given us

For through its lessons do the trees within the forest
become like unto the Gods and spirits of an ancient land...

the means whereby to write and keep this knowledge true.

Now Ogma did come unto the sacred Oak and then did he write the seven vowels we speak upon its bark, and this he did by taking forth his blade and making cuts across a line that he hath marked upon the wood. And seven letters within the Alphabet did he then create upon the Oak.

Then did he create other letters which belong to different trees. For he hath fashioned the letter 'B' from Beith, which we call Birch, and 'L' from Luis – which is our sacred Rowan tree or Mountain Ash. And 'D' hath sprung forth from Duir, the Oak of Fate, and 'N' from Nuin which is the Ash from which we make our spears. And 'C' from Coll, which is the Hazel in the woods, and 'F' from Fearn which is the Alder we employ to make our shields. As so it did follow that twenty oghams did come forth, and then another five besides, and so it was that a secret Alphabet of the Trees hath come to be. And all of these letters hath Ogma formed by making cuts upon the tree – some marks above the line, and some below, and some upon an angle, and five with other markings that I show you here.

And then hath colours to these letters been assigned – by the bards who do protect the Wisdom of the Ancient Ones. For then have these bards gone forth and taken dyes from the berries and the bark and the seeds that these trees do bear. And so by the colours of their cloaks, which hath been dyed with juices from these

trees, so then shall the bards come to know the rank and symbol that they doth present one unto the other. For amongst the Chieftain Trees are the Oak and Hazel, Ash, Yew and Fir. And then are there Peasant Trees and amongst them are the Alder, Willow, Birch and Elm. And there are trees we know as Shrubs, which do include amongst their number the Blackthorn, Elder, Spindletree and Honeysuckle, and there are Herbs, like Broom and Heather and Gorse – or Furze as some have known it. And the mystic colour of Oak hath been ascribed as dark brown, and the colour of Ash is sea-green, and Yew is earth-red. And as its name doth suggest, Hazel is known as orange-brown, and Fir is grey and Gorse is like the colour of the sand. Thus have we come to know the secret colours which are assigned unto the Alphabet of Trees.

Then, too, have the metals been linked unto the vowels so that 'A' hath become known by silver, 'E' by tin, 'I' by iron and lead, 'O' by gold, and 'U' by copper. And certain trees are ruled by the Signs which doth command a path within the Heavens so that 'L' hath become the letter of Virgo, and 'F' of Leo, and 'S' of Aries. And certain birds, too, hath been linked unto the Alphabet of Trees so that 'L' is one with the Duck, and 'S' hath become the Hawk and 'T' hath been linked unto the Starling. And these things have I lain before you here within this Book of Magick, these secrets here to keep.

The Ogham Alphabet and its Signs

Ogham	Letter	Irish Name	Our Tree Nam
	B	Beith	Birch
	L	Luis	Rowan
	F,V	Fearn	Alder
	S	Saille	Willow
	N	Nuin	Ash
	h	huathe	hawthorn
	d	duir	Oak
	T	Tinne	holly
	C,K	Coll	hazel
	q	Quert	Wild Apple
	m	Muinn	Vine or Bramble
	G	Gort	Ivy
	NG	Ngetal	Broom, Juniper
	STR/SS/ST/Z	Straif	Blackthorn, Wild Plum
	R	Ruis	Elder
	A	Ailm	Silver Fir, Pine
	O	Onn	Gorse. Furze
	U	Ur	heather
	E	Edhadh	Aspen
	I,J,Y	Ido	Yew
	EA,Ch	Ebhadh	Aspen
	OI,Th	Oir	Spindletree
	UI/P	Uileand	honeysuckle
	IO/IA	Iphin	Gooseberry
	AE	Phagos	Beech

Colour	Zodiac Ruler	Bird
White	–	Pheasant
Dark Grey	Virgo	Duck
Crimson	Leo	Gull
Yellow/Pink	Aries	Hawk
Blue-green	Aquarius	Snipe
Black	Libra	Crow
Dark Brown	Scorpio	Wren
Scarlet	Cancer	Starling
Orange-brown	Taurus	Crane
Apple Green	–	-
Purple	Sagattarius	Titmouse
Blue /Light Blue	Capricorn	Mute Swan
Light Yellow-green	Pisces	Goose
Orange-red	–	-
Red	Gemini	Rook
Grey		
Gold, sand		
Light Green		
Light Yellow		
Earth Red		
Green		
Red		
Doe Red		
Whitish Grey		
Black, White		

DIVINING WITH THE OGHAMS

ow must I tell you how these oghams may indeed be used to conjure future things – to lay before you what will come to pass. For in this way shall you become skilled and learned in the mystic ways of prophecy.

For now shall you go unto the woods and there shall you gather straight branches of Oak – for Oak is known as the Lord of all Trees, and doth all trees embrace. And from these branches shall you cut smaller staves of wood and square them off upon one side, so you may mark a single letter from the Alphabet of Trees upon each stave in turn.

And when the time doth arise for divining what is yet to come, then shall you take yourself away unto a quiet place – to your private chamber or to your secret circle in the woods, and there shall you lay the twenty-five ogham staves upon the ground. And now, with eyes closed, shall you reach forward and collect seven of these staves and hold them close with both hands. And do this as you form within your mind the question you would ask that doth pertain to future times and places – for

the oghams shall give an answer to these things. And now cast these seven staves before you on the ground. And it shall come to pass that those staves that come to rest close at hand do speak of the present, and those that are further from your reach do speak of things and times which yet lie within the future, and have not yet come to pass. And staves which cross or touch each other — these staves do have a strong and clear connection, one upon the other, and thus are their meanings linked. For when you cast your eye upon the staves, and see the mystic letters marked upon them thus, then shall you know the meaning of the oracle you have cast. For these meanings have I written here, within this Book of Magick — for your guidance and your knowledge in this world. And whereof certain matters will yet come to be.

The Meaning of the Oghams in Divination

ᛒ	Beith	There shall be new beginnings, for now shall you change your ways
ᚂ	Luis	Now must you seek protection against the control of others over you
ꜰ,ᴠ	Fearn	Now need you guidance to make your true choices upon the mystic path
ꜱ	Saille	Now shall you gain balance within your life
ɴ	Nuin	Now you are linked steadfast unto something that will surely come to pass
ᚆ	Huathe	Now shall you be held back for a certain time
ᚇ	Duir	You gain great strength and are no longer afraid
ᴛ	Tinne	You muster courage to face troubles which lie ahead
ᴄ,ᴋ	Coll	Now will you gain power and vision for your work
ꞯ	Quert	Now must a choice of great import be made
ᚋ	Muinn	Take quiet unto yourself for now shall you be stronger within your soul

G	Gort	Inquire of your soul, lest you taketh the wrong path
NG	Ngetal	Hurt and upset doth lie ahead
STR,Z	Straif	You do not wish to see the truth that hath cometh before you
R	Ruis	Now have you come to the end of that which doth concern thee
A	Ailm	Take due care with the choices that you now must make
O	Onn	Now hath arisen something to lead your life unto a new and different path
U	Ur	Healing of the spirit shall come unto your life
E	Edhadh	Fears and doubts doth come full and fast upon thee
I,J,Y	Ido	Now shall your life take a quite different turn
EA,CH	Ebhadh	Now may you overcome false ideas thou hast held from the past
OI,TH	Oir	Complete your tasks now, before you move forward unto new ones
UI, P	Uileand	Now must you proceed with all due care
IO, IA	Iphin	Soon will new tidings come unto your life
AE	Phagos	Indeed, soon will you travel afar

OTHER MEANS
WHEREBY YOU MAY
COME TO KNOW THE
FUTURE

@

Yet is it also true that we may divine what the future doth portend, through other means as well. For oft have I come unto the waters of a secret, swiftly flowing stream, and here through my cunning and my craft have I taken from the waters a fine and noble salmon – which is in truth a creature that doth embody sacred wisdom and hidden knowing. And I have brought this fine and noble fish in a pail of river water and sanctified it within the magick circle – giving my blessings unto the Ancient Ones who doth watch over the Four Quarters. And then hath this noble fish offered of its soul unto the God of Water and all his cupbearers, and I have eaten from its flesh within the sacred circle to partake of its wisdom and its knowing.

For by this rite may we recall the Sacred Well of Segais, which is for all a source of Great Wisdom. Nine Hazel trees grow beside this sacred well and it is said that each and every year these Hazel trees do blossom

...we may divine what the future doth portend,
through other means as well...

and in due time release their magick nuts unto the well. And then doth the noble salmon come forth to feed upon the nuts which drop therein.

And when it cometh to pass that we partake of the flesh of the noble salmon within the magick circle, and with blessings duly given unto the Gods of the Four Quarters, then may we ask concerning certain things which are to come, and then will wisdom and knowing be granted unto us, through the eating of this mystic salmon – for this knowledge cometh from the realms of Otherworld.

And another path in prophecy have I also learned. For through a knowledge of the clouds may we also come to know what yet shall come to pass. Yet must you wait until the coming of Full Moon, and also for a time when clouds do gather large and full within the sky. Then, as Father Sun doth drop low unto the earth and the clouds are yet ablaze with fire, then within the early hours of evening as our fair Lady of the Moon doth soon rise up to shine her face upon the world, then shall you take a small dish and take it unto a swiftly flowing stream. Thence shall you fill it with the waters from this place and take yourself quietly unto your secret mystic place within the woods.

And there within the magick circle and after making due offerings unto the Ancient Ones of the Four Quarters and to our Lady of the Moon, than shall you place this dish of water upon the sacred earth. And as you gazeth down into the dish with quiet resolve, now may you observe the glowing clouds through the mirror of the water. Ask now your question of the future, and call the Ancient Ones of Otherworld to grant an answer through your soul.

And now shall you gently place the bowl aside and lay you down upon your back within the magick circle – looking up unto the Moon-lit sky above. And as surely as the fire doth leave these clouds behind with the setting of the sun, now will the Moon-lit clouds assume new and wondrous shapes before you – and the faces of those who are both known and unknown will rise up within your gaze. And at this time will your question of the future times be answered by Our Lady of the Moon. For she doth shine her wise light upon us and shares her secrets in the darkness of the night.

SUMMONING A LOVER

ou must surely know within yourself that to attract a lover you must first feel the welling up of love within yourself. This surge of love you then can send forth into the world through your magick, to seek the lover who will in truth become your heart's desire.

Choose for this enchantment the cycle of the Full or Waxing Moon – for it is at this time that magick doth reap its richest rewards. And in your private and sanctified place – which may yet be within a secret grove amidst the Oaks or in a quiet and private place within your own chamber – there must you first fashion the magick circle in the way that I have told you – by inscribing it upon the ground, or making it upon your wooden floor with a ring of special stones that you have taken for this purpose from the banks of a river or from within a mountain stream. For love is like a river whose eddies do flow down upon the mountainside seeking firm and strong banks to cradle and hold the river-current within their arms. Thus is the magick of love ruled by Water, and surely will you find your heart's fulfilment in this way:

For in this rite shall you wear only those clothes that would entice your lover, and perhaps you may be clad in no clothes whatever – 'sky-clad' as the Ancient Ones

...you must first feel the welling up of love within yourself...

have called it. Come now unto your sacred space with all your tools of magick – your dagger, wand, cup and pentacle – and bring too a chalice or glass bowl filled unto the brim with pure spring water. Bring also with you red roses – for these are flowers of love. But take care too to cut away the small thorns which do resteth firm upon the stem, and do this before you come unto the magick circle, for a thorn-prick will surely cast your thoughts far from your magick quest!

Once you have come unto the magick circle, now shall you honour the Four Directions, and at each point give your blessings unto the Holy Ones. Place now your metal dagger in the East, the realm of Air – for this is surely the quarter of the rising Moon. In the South, the realm of Fire, place your magick wooden wand, and in the West – the realm of Water, a small bowl of spring water. Finally, must you place your metal pentacle in the North, to honour Earth. On your altar place a dish of salt, the special chalice for your love-magick, and a small dish for burning incense if you desire it. And here too may you place any magick gemstones which you have chosen for the task.

Now shall you build the magick of the circle by dancing your love unto the Four Quarters. Commencing now within the East and clasping a rose unto your heart, now shall you intone these words:

I touch Love *(and take delight in the lustrous texture which is found within the petals)*

Dancing deosil and with a free and spiralling motion now do you come unto the South, where, again you hold the rose unto your heart and say:

I see love coming (for the rose doth impart your deep yearning for a loving partner)

Dancing still further around your magick circle come now unto the West, where again you hold the rose unto your heart and say:

I taste love (and you kiss the petals of the rose)

And then do you dance unto the North and, drawing the rose close to your face, say:

I smell the sweet scent of love (for now you drink in the beautiful scent of the rose)

Coming now unto the centre of the magick circle and relecting deep upon the purpose of your love, now shall you intone these words:

Love is before me

Love is behind me

Love is beside me

Love is above me

Love is below me

Love is within me

Now cometh that time within your enchantment when you shall summon into a likeness before you, the true form of your heart's desire:

Taking now the chalice within your hand and facing unto the East, gaze now into the crystalline waters. For you this vessel doth now become a mirror unto the soul and a mirror unto the world.

Gaze deeply now within the waters, hold long and true unto your heart's intent, and call for the Mistress of the Waters to guide you in your quest. And in a certain time a mist will come upon the surface of the water, and that mist will rise up all around you, and fill your heart and soul with enchantment. Now, with all your powers of magickal intent, have it come to pass that the lover you most desire should appear before you – for you shall conjure this person into your heart's eye in every fine respect. Notice too that you embrace, taking her lovingly within your arms. And see before you the world in which you both would dwell. Hold now these thoughts and feelings deep within you and do conjure and will them thus to be. Then take your peace, resting thoughtfully upon the love you have evoked, and in due course take your leave of the magick circle in the way I have instructed you.

For by working magick in this way, then will the love which is your heart's desire find its way to come unto your life. And perchance as many know, thus did I conjure the fair and lovely Vivian to come within my heart and soul in just this way, and so was I drawn through the laws of magickal enchantment to meet and love her in the wondrous Forest of Broceliande.

...call for the Mistress of the Waters to guide you in your quest...

BONDING YOUR LOVE
WITH CANDLE MAGICK

@

Once your lover has come to you in this way, and doth reside within your heart, and you do hold this love dear within your life, now must you take all care to keep it strong and true:

Take a perfect apple and share it with your loved one, taking bites by turn. From the apple's core now take nine seeds, seal them in a pouch, and sleep with it beneath your pillow for the first three nights of the waxing moon. And if you do indeed sleep peacefully and without dreams of anguish that rise up from your soul, then may you proceed still further with this magick.

During the daylight hours at this time, seek out a candle and place it in a special candlestick. The candle's shape and colour must be pleasing to the eye – the very essence of your love.

On the sixth night of the waxing moon, then shall you assemble the apple seeds, the candle and its holder, and also a small amount of vegetable oil, a handful of leaves that you have gathered from a birch tree, and two small pans. Do ensure you are alone, for no-one should enter your room as you work within.

Draw now a small quantity of water and heat it within the pan until it is just warm. Hold the candle base within the warm water until the wax is then soft enough to receive the sharp end of an apple seed. Then surely press each apple seed into the wax, one by one, until all nine are firmly there in place. And if your room is cool, do continue to dip the bottom of the candle within the warm water so that the wax will remain soft enough to receive each seed in turn. Whilst the candle end is still soft, permit the candle to cool.

Now immerse the birch leaves in oil which you have gently warmed and allow them to steep within the second pan. Ease the candle from the holder and anoint it thus: Apply birch oil with your forefinger from the centre of the candle to the wick's end and back to the base until the entire surface is lightly coated. Now can you replace the candle in its holder and hide it away within a cupboard or a closet. And it must be stored upright and in a dark place.

Now indeed may the candle be lit whenever the need arises. For if your beloved faceth danger or has gone away on a journey, or there is strife or anxiety, then shall it serve you well. It will be a comfort and a safeguard of your love. Take care never to allow any person to light this candle once it hath become a symbol of the union of your love. And should this by some ill chance occur, make haste then to melt out the nine apple seeds, and prepare another candle.

FURTHER KNOWLEDGE CONCERNING CANDLE MAGICK

Let me now instruct you further concerning the powers of candle magick, for this is surely a wondrous aid upon the mystic path. For by now must you know that a candle through its light doth embody all that is true and valiant within your heart . And when a candle doth burn with its flame uplifted to the sky, then may you not hide your true desires from the Ancient Ones who watch over us with the passing of the hours and days. For the candle's flame doth provide guidance upon the path we travel and then are dark shadows cast aside. And the colour of the candle we have chosen for our magick purpose doth provide a sign of our true intent, for there are candles apt for all mystic tasks within this world.

And this magick rite may you recall, for it doth good fortune bring: Sit you now within your magick circle and do free your soul to take its flight amidst the glowing flame of the candle you have lit. And when your soul is filled with light, may you then become like unto the candle — a beacon for the wise and true. Take now a piece of parchment and inscribe upon it

your magick spell. Read now this spell three times, then cast the parchment forth into the flame. And say these words:

UNTO YOUR REALM, GREAT DANA, I DO COMMIT THIS SPELL

DO BRING ITS RICH REWARDS TO ME, SO FOR TO HELP ME IN MY TASK

BY ALL THE STRENGTH OF MOON AND SUN

BY ALL THE STRENGTH OF SACRED OAK

BY ALL THE STRENGTH OF THE GREAT GODDESS, FAIR LADY OF THE

FLOWERS AND HER LOVER THE HORNED GOD, LORD OF ANIMALS...

SO MAY THIS SPELL BE MANIFEST FOR ME

Know always that to cause increase in your life, whether of abundance, good health or good tidings alike , then shall such spells be cast during the waxing of the Moon, and for best effect when the Moon is full. And to cause a reverse, or to remove some ill that hath befallen thee, do make this magick at the time of waning Moon – and for best effect at New Moon when the Lady of the Night doth veil herself in darkness.

And then may these words comfort you:

CANDLE OF POWER, CANDLE OF MIGHT

DO GRANT MY WISH UPON THIS NIGHT

MAY POWER FLOW FROM CANDLE-FIRE

AND BRING TO ME MY HEART' S DESIRE

MY WORDS ARE STRONG, MY CAUSE IS WON

I NOW DECLARE THIS SPELL IS DONE

And here are different coloured candles that you may then take to aid your magick purpose:

WHITE: This colour doth pertain to all that is pure in spirit and to the noble directions that you do seek within your life

BLACK: This colour shall be used to undo the dark forces that doth assail you. So too may it reverse or release that which hath constricted you

RED: This colour is full with the energy of life that hath been bestowed by the Ancient Ones and it doth give power and strength and good health

PINK: For this colour is a colour of love that doth unite two people, and so too may it also serve to heal your spirit

YELLOW: This colour doth reflect the power of your mind to make good reason and thence go forth unto the world charged with strength and vision

ORANGE: For this colour doth signify to power of one thing to attract another and also to change bad luck unto good fortune

Green: Like the colour of newly risen grass in Spring, this colour doth signify new growth, abundance and success within your life

Blue: For this colour doth call forth the power of truth and wisdom upon the mystic path. So too may it also serve you well to summon good health and peace unto your life

Purple: This colour must you employ to call the most noble visions to dwell within your soul. For then shall the Gods and spirits come amongst you to bestow their gifts of grace and drive away the demons that might deceive you

Brown: For this colour doth signify good fortune in the ways of wealth upon this Earth

Gold: This colour doth bestow good fortune – abundance both within this world and yet also blessings which shall lead you forth unto the Otherworld to come

Silver: This colour doth banish powers of darkness and may also serve to honour Our Lady of the Moon who doth uplift us all with her gifts of magick vision

how you may attract wealth through magick means

Some hath proclaimed that to make magick for wealth doth offend the Gods and spirits alike and speaking for myself I have oft reflected deep upon these things. And yet do I believe within my heart that our intent within the ways of magick is of the highest import. For if you do need good assets to assist your learning or your travail abroad, or yet some other worthy cause, then may a spell cast for wealth be employed with good intent. And yet should you wish for wealth and good fortune to flow into your life for selfish pleasure and your merriment alone, then may this magick turn against you, and instead of wealth may loss or injury bring within its wake. So shall you be sure indeed that within your soul are found both truth and good intent, for the Spirit is not fooled in matters such as these.

As well you know, the waxing Moon doth provide the most propitious time for magick of abundance, and Full Moon – as I have said – is indeed the best eve of all, for to call good fortune forth unto your life. Take then your

Hold deep and true within your heart
the full intent that doth accompany your wish for wealth...

cauldron – half-filled with water – into the magick circle and anoint the Four Quarters as you have learned in conjuring the ways of love. And make haste to light brown candles at each of the Four Quarters for this doth bring abundance to the Earthly realm.

Then within your cauldron make haste to place a silver coin so that the sweet beams cast by our Lady of the Moon doth reflect her radiant face through these waters. Sweep now your hands above the surface of the water which resteth in the cauldron – for in this way do you gather unto yourself all the silver of the Moon – and say these words:

Fair Lady of the Moon

Bring unto me wealth right soon

Do fill my hands with silver and with gold

Enrich my life with all a purse may hold

Say these words thrice, and then – after you have departed the magick circle and erased it from the earth – pour the water from the cauldron down upon the ground.

So too may you increase the power of this magick spell forthwith with candle magick. For on the Sunday that followeth this Full Moon, light within your chamber a golden candle – for gold doth represent all that is rich and glorious and abundant. Hold deep and true within your heart the full intent that doth accompany your wish for wealth, and say these words:

Goddess of Plenty

Bringer of fine bounty

I do beseech you now

To listen to these words of mine

For a worthy task I do require this wealth

And so do hear my call and upon me this wealth bestow

O Great Goddess of Plenty

Repeat these words with good intent each Sunday morning before a golden candle until wealth and abundance doth appear within your life.

how to find something which was lost

❂

f it has come to pass that some object which
you do value or admire is lost and you know
not what hath become of it, then shall you
perform a certain magick wherefore to learn its
whereabouts. And you must surely know that for this
purpose must you learn the art of scrying – for in this
way may you divine the place where lost things may yet
be found.

And there are two ways to scry which yet are dear to
me. One useth Fire whilst the other doth employ Water
– and both to good effect.

For Fire, shall you take a candle, and its colour shall
be like unto the purpose of your quest, as I have told
you. And during the quietness of the evening, now shall
you take yourself away unto your chamber and light the
candle – for to still your mind and gaze upon its flame.
And then shall you enter deep within the spirit-vision
and your quest shall beginneth then. And may you hold
within your mind these thoughts and intent:

And then must you make your prayer to her,
for to help retrieve that which hath gone astray...

Mystic flame, you dance within the night

Mystic flame, you spread your kindly light

Bring before me what I need to see

Bring before me what I need to see

Then in due time, and with patience, and within the quietness of the night, shall the object present itself unto you within flames of the candle and within the spirit-vision which doth reveal all things. For you do have a bond indeed – you do love and treasure that which you have lost – and then shall it return itself to you.

And so too may objects which have gone astray be revealed through the magick of Water.

At the time of Full Moon take yourself away to your secret place which resteth amongst the sacred oaks, and with you take a black bowl which yet is without design or embellishment or other colours which doth distract the eye. And fill this bowl full with water from a spring or creek.

Within the bowl shall you place a small crystal or coin of silver and then shall you place the bowl upon the earth so that it doth allow the beams from our Lady of the Moon to fall full upon the surface of the water. And perhaps some incense shall you also burn, to lift up your spirit unto the Lady of the Moon as a greeting. And then must you make your prayer to her, for to help retrieve that which hath gone astray:

By the magick of the Moon, by faery spell

By the mysteries which here do dwell

Dreams, desires and mystery might

Borne on moonbeam's silver light

Come now before me in my mystic bowl

For once the beams of the Full Moon hath reacheth down and lit the crystal or the silver coin within your bowl, then do many forms flit and swim within the dark waters therein, and bring themselves to view. And with patience and with trust, and in good time, then shall the missing object come to view — for you shall see it there within your mystic bowl and know henceforth how you may recover it whence it came.

TO CAST ASIDE MISFORTUNE AND GATHER UNTO YOURSELF GOOD LUCK

@

Full well you know if you have already made your way upon the mystic path that the Rowan tree is honoured among my people, for evil and bad fortune doth it dispel.

Now, when summer hath come unto its height and the Rowan tree is full-laden with ripe red fruit, find you first a branch that reacheth unto the South. Take this branch within your grasp and now, with light touch, shake upon the tree to cause four berries to fall. Take these up, and gather also four leaves from the very same branch – and then make haste with them, for to bring them back unto your chamber. Now make you a fire within your hearth, of birch and apple wood, and when the fire blazeth with red and golden flame, cast forth a single rowan berry and its leaf, unto the heart of the fire forthwith. And say these words:

...cast forth a single rowan berry unto the fire...

VIRTUE BE MINE, AS FROM THIS TREE

BEWARE THE FIRE I CAST AT THEE

Now take you a second berry and its leaf, and consign these too unto the flames:
And say these words:

WISDOM IS MINE, AS FROM THIS TREE

BEWARE THE FIRE I CAST AT THEE

And now take you a third berry and its leaf, and cast them forth unto the fire. And say these words:

POWER IS MINE, AS FROM THIS TREE

BEWARE THE FIRE I CAST AT THEE

Now, in due time, take the fourth berry and its leaf and place them within an iron pot. Roast this pot slowly over the fire until the berry and its leaf have become dry and black with heat, and then cool them on the ground. Place them now within a red cloth and bury this magick charm within the earth and yet near the doorway which leadeth into your house – for then shall no harm befall thee. For evil-doers shall withdraw themselves from its presence should they come unto this place.

...then shall no harm befall thee...

TO MAKE MISCHIEF AGAINST THOSE THAT OFFENDETH THEE, AND ALSO HOW TO PLACE A CURSE UPON YOUR ENEMIES

@

Well may you know that magick may be used against those who doth offend thee, or who hath wrought harm or evil against you in this world. And yet know always that magick hath its own truth and virtue, and shall not with whimsy or trite reason be abused. Make heed to respect it always and know that rites cast against another may indeed return with threefold strength against oneself – if not the cause be true. Know too that magick may have different strengths and potencies – then shall you choose a spell or rite that doth reflect the time and the occasion forthwith.

For here is a spell that shall cause mischief to befall another, and well may he rue the day that he crossed your path with ill intent:

Well may you know that magick may be
used against those who doth offend thee...

Gather now from all corners of your chamber, all the cobwebs that you can muster and place them in a pile upon a black cloth which you have brought for this purpose. Take then a dead fly or some other loathsome insect and place it within the very centre of the entangled webs. And now write the name of your enemy together with these words upon a parchment:

North, South, East, West
Spider's web shall bind him best
East, West, North, South
Trap his limbs and bond his mouth
Seal his eyes and choke his breath
And make him fear he's bound for death

Now take this parchment forthwith and fold it four times, then wrap it together with the dead insect and the cobwebs in the black cloth, making them into a small black bag. Bind this bag with a cord and hang it from the ceiling of your chamber. Do not disturb it for some days, for then a thick coat of dust will form upon it. When it is covered with a coat of dust in this way, take the bag down from the ceiling and bury it within the earth. Then may it work its binding effect upon your enemy forever.... until you have cause to remove it from the earth.

Should you wish to make your magick stronger still, wait until the waning Moon hath come into the sky, and

on the evening of your rite bring your cauldron unto your altar within the magick circle. Make a blazing fire forthwith and burn heather then, for to protect you against your enemies. Place the cauldron between two black candles and place a third black candle at the midpoint in the Northern quarter. Burn now an incense of protection – St Johns Wort, Hazel, Wintersweet or Rowan – and gather unto your side a parchment with the names of your enemies inscribed. If you know not who your enemy be but feel that evil doth come against you from all sides, write then 'All mine enemies...' upon the parchment.

Cast forth basil and elder flowers unto the flames within the cauldron and say these words with all the force and might that you can muster:

    Bubble, bubble...cauldron bubble

    Burn this evil, burn the trouble

Now take the parchment that doth bear the names of your enemies, light it from the black candle in the North and cast it forth unto the flames that riseth up within the cauldron. Take up your mystic wand, wave it forth above the pot of fire, and do then recite these words:

    Darkness ends, the rite is done

    Light has come...my fight is won

145

In due time, when the blaze hath receded, take the ashes from the pot and cast them unto the winds.

I also share with you this curse which I hath learnt from mine own enemies – from the Saxons who did come unto this land with Vortigern and who now are vanquished. And yet is the curse a potent one, for I have used it oft against those who would come against me with grave intent:

I curse ye by a right line, a crooked line,

a simple and a broken.

By flame, by wind, by a mass, by rain, by clay.

By a flying thing, by a creeping thing, by a serpent,

By an eye, by a hand, by a foot,

By a crown, by a cross, by a sword and by a scourge

I curse thee…

Cast forth basil and elder flowers unto the flames
within the cauldron..

how to Become invisible

Now surely do you know already that all that exists in life doth consist in varying degrees of Earth, Water, Fire and Air and that Spirit doth sustain us all – for Spirit in truth is all that doth exist.

And if we wish to become invisible, then must we return to Spirit, for then are we in truth without form and may become anything we would wish – thence to take an animal's appearance, or to become like unto a flower, or like a sacred tree or to become any other thing or creature that doth suit our purpose.

Then must we take ourself away unto a quiet place within the depths of night, and here shall we quieten ourselves and take ourselves far away into the inner vision of our souls. And then when we have become quiet and deep wthin ourselves, then shall we light a white candle which doth represent the Spirit, and then shall we fix our gaze intently upon its fulgent glow, becoming one within its light.

And now shall we remember that our body – our outward form that we do show unto this world – is like unto the Earth, for our body doth clothe our soul. And

...we are Water through and through, and Water have we become...

now shall we dissolve our bodies into Water and hold true within our spirit-vision that our soul doth flow forth from the confines of the body and doth Otherworld embrace. And so we take now the form of Water in our spirit-vision and we are Water through and through, and Water have we become.

And now that we have become one with Water, now shall we direct our deepest thoughts to becoming one with Fire. And as fire heateth water within a bowl and the water doth rise up into the sky as vapour, so then shall we become like unto the vapour which Water doth become. And we are one with it, and now too do we rise up like steam unto the sky, and we then may become one in turn with Air.

For now have we become like unto the clouds that do float like gentle birds across the sky. And yet clouds do float away, almost into nothingness. And so are we now like unto clouds that do Air embrace, and yet are we ready to dissolve our souls within the Spirit that doth embraceth All Things That Are.

And so it is that in the spirit-vision our soul doth merge its very being within the sacred Spirit and in this way do we come to know the Mystery that doth give us life and form within this world. For now are we at the very heart of All That Is, and then are we contained within our bodies no further, and we have no form to hold unto. For we are now invisible to human gaze – and yet still we are, for still we live and see. Indeed, we

know that we are anything that could ever be. And we are like unto the Gods.

For this magick secret is well known amongst the Ancient Ones and doth the mystic quest embrace. For how could it be that the Great Dana, Mother of the Gods, could become like unto a hare? Or that Morrigu could yet become a raven or an eel? Or that Aige might become one with a fawn, and Dechtire like a swan, and Lord Cernunnos like unto a fox or badger, wolf or stag, and Muanna like unto a crane? Or that the great Dagda – Lord of Life and Death, whom we honour at Samhain – might transform himself into a sacred Oak or become a living harp amongst us all? For the Ancient Ones hath learnt to make these changes well, and their secret doth rest with those who through magick have come to know and love these mystic ways. For when you do truly know through the magick arts of the Ancient Ones how you may become invisible before the human gaze, and how you may transform yourself into another form, then have you become a master of the Craft.

how to fly in the spirit-vision

@

or it has always been since ancient times that wise wizards and witches who doth have the mystic power within their grasp could fly across the sky and then take themselves unto the Otherworld and midst the Ancient Ones who do dwell within the hallowed realms beyond the Veil of Mist. And yet amongst the commonfolk many have been seized with fear on learning this, and then have asked: how could this be, that through wizardry and magick that one may come to fly unto the heavens as if he were a bird? And so now will I tell you of these things.

For, as I have said, first must you come unto a quiet place within the midst of night and in this place prepare a resting place within your circle of magick and beneath the gaze of the Guardians of the Four Quarters so that your body may yet slumber undisturbed. And then shall you once again prepare to take yourself again from Earth unto Water and thence unto Fire and unto Air — and then unto the form of the wise raven who doth take its flight across the skies.

And now, as you resteth quiet upon the ground,

perhaps almost to the edge of slumber and yet with your mind and vision ever watchful, call now for the Ancient Ones to fill your body with the sacred light that doth come forth from the Cauldron of the Wise, this light for to give you strength and throw its welcome light upon the mystic path of your travail. And now as this light doth fill your body and your heart, and doth illumine your soul forthwith to fly, then once more shall you feel your body pass from Earth and dissolve within the Water, and reach out then unto the further shores. And now shall you feel the inner Fire which all followers upon the mystic path do conjure forth to rise within themselves – from within the cauldron that hath become the heart's desire – and now shall you make ready to rise up into the Air like the ever curling streams of vapour that do rise up from the cauldron and yield their flow unto the stars. Now shall you shape your form to take unto yourself the visage of the wise raven. And as you do call upon Lord Dagda, who art Lord of Life and Death and who doth guard the door to Otherworld, that he might aid you in this task – so too shall you conjure in your own mind's vision that a beak hath formed between your eyes, that feathers do now come forth upon your breast and from your flanks, and from your arms hath strong and glorious wings emerged. And you do feel the urge strong within your heart that now shall you fly unto the heavens, and a mystic force hath come unto your strong and glorious wings and the keen vision

of the raven hath come unto your eyes. And now do you rise up in flight for thou hast become the sacred raven, and now may you look downwards to see your human form beneath, slumbering all the while upon the earth whilst your soul shall yet take flight within the spirit-vision.

And now shall you hold firm within your heart the strong desire in magick which hath brought you forth, and then with the cawing of the raven and the power of magick in your soul as you do fly with all your heart's desire, then shall you make your way unto the Ancient Ones – the wise and shining ones who do dwell beyond the Veil of Mist. For nothing now may hold you back upon your quest, and now do you seize your freedom with your wings, and so may you fly unto the Gods and dwell amongst them, their sacred knowing to receive.

And then when you have travailed amongst these Ancient Ones and gloried in their light, and hath their knowledge and their mystic gifts received, then may you turn in flight once more and take yourself back unto the night skies of the homeland and to the magick circle whence your slumbering form still resteth upon the ground. And now as surely as you hath the Air embraced, so too will Fire once more rise up within your human heart – for the torch of sacred things hath been lit by the Gods – and then do the Waters of Life flow amidst the embers of the Fire and draw you back within the mystic stream that doth these faculties enrich. And

now surely do these waters flow upon the Earth and so too do you dissolve your raven form and become yet again one within the human shape that slumbers on the ground. And ever gently, and in the depths of quiet, do you return to human form. And in good time shall you arise within that mystic circle and give your thanks and praise unto Lord Dagda and his host of Gods and spirits, for the gifts they have bestowed.

Upon the coming of the dawn, then shall you erase this magick circle from the face of the earth and take yourself away. And then shall you spend much time in deep reflection, and once again give thanks unto the Ancient Ones for the ways in magick that hath been granted unto you, and which are surely blessed and sacred in this world. For magick is known in truth as the Path of the Wise, and so it is that I do bequeath this book henceforth unto your watchful care, so that this knowledge be not lost or scattered forth unto the wind.

HERE ENDETH

THIS BOOK

OF MAGICK...

The Author

Nevill Drury was born in Hastings in 1947 and was inspired as a child by the fantasy illustrations of Arthur Rackham and Edmund Dulac, which evoked a timeless feeling of magic and the 'Otherworld'. Still fascinated by this genre, he has also been influenced by the mystical tales of Lord Dunsany and Arthur Machen, which have left an enduring mark on his own writing.

Since the release of his first book, *The Search for Abraxas*, in 1972, Nevill Drury has continued to research and publish books on the western esoteric tradition and has specialised in the fields of magic, mythology, shamanism and visionary states of consciousness. His most recent books include *The Elements of Shamanism*, *The Visionary Human*, *Pan's Daughter* and *Echoes from the Void*. He holds a Masters degree in anthropology and is the Publishing Director of a company specialising in books on contemporary Australian and international art.

The Illustrator

LINDA GARLAND lives in Cornwall and is renowned internationally for her fantasy illustrations – which have appeared in calendars and on numerous book jackets, posters and cards. Linda is especially well known for her Goddess paintings, but also draws on Symbolist, Pre-Raphaelite and Classical influences. She works with her husband Roger Garland, who is also a well-known illustrator, and a collection of their artwork was recently published with the title *Garlands of Fantasy*.

MetroBooks

An Imprint of Friedman/Fairfax Publishers

This edition published by MetroBooks by arrangement with Lansdowne Publishing

ISBN 1-5866-3754-1

1 3 5 7 9 10 8 6 4 2

For bulk purchases and special sales, please contact:
Friedman/Fairfax Publishers
Attention: Sales Department
230 Fifth Avenue, Suite 700
New York, NY 10001
212/685-6610 FAX 212/685-3916

Visit our website:
www.metrobooks.com

First Published in 1996
Designer: Robyn Latimer

Set in Bernhard Modern and Macedon on QuarkXpress
Printed in Hong Kong by South China Printing